SACRED PLACES

A Guide to the Civil Rights Sites
in Atlanta, Georgia

Harry G. Lefever and Michael C. Page

Mercer University Press, 2008

MERCER

ISBN 978-0-88146-121-3
MUP/P379

Mercer University Press
1400 Coleman Avenue
Macon, Georgia 31207

First Edition.

Book design by Burt and Burt Studio

∞The paper used in this publication meets the minimum
requirements of American National Standard for Information
Sciences—Permanence of Paper for Printed Library Materials,
ANSI Z39.48-1992.

Library of Congress Cataloging-in-Publication Data

Lefever, Harry G.
Sacred places: A Guide to the Civil Rights Sites in Atlanta, Georgia
Harry G. Lefever and Michael C. Page.
p. cm.
Includes bibliographical references and index
ISBN-13: 978-0-88146-121-3   ISBN-10: 0-88146-121-0
pbk.: alk. paper
1. Civil rights movements–Georgia–Atlanta–History–20th century
2. African Americans–Civil rights–Georgia–Atlanta
3. Atlanta (Ga.)–Race relations–History–20th century
4. Atlanta (Ga.)–Description and travel
5. Atlanta (Georgia)–History
I. Page, Michael C. II. Title.
JC599.U52G445 2008
323.1196'0730758231–dc22
2008042335

Four Tours

● ● ● ●

● ● ● ●

⬡ ⬡ ⬡ ⬢

Tour Four: Four Scattered Sites 133

Foreword

I was struck by the title of this book. It is a meaningful walk through the pages and places of history. It is a guide to the cornerstones of the civil rights movement in Atlanta. But you may be asking, what is it about the Butler Street YMCA, the Atlanta Life Insurance Company, or even Ebenezer Baptist Church that makes them sacred places? What you will discover when you walk these roads of history is that the actions of everyday citizens—people just like you and me—transformed these plain, ordinary buildings into monuments of democracy.

The United States was not founded on long-standing tradition or by the agreement of kings. It was not created by mandate or decree. It is a nation founded upon ideals, on profound philosophical concepts that we have spent generations and centuries trying to fulfill.

The Declaration of Independence affirms that the equality of all mankind is self-evident. It says there are certain inherent rights, granted by God, which cannot be separated from our humanity—life, liberty, and the pursuit of happiness. And as a nation we believe no law, no president, no member of Congress, no city councilperson or police officer, no employer or employee, no citizen or resident should violate these principles. It is these values that have made this nation a symbol of freedom around the world and have established our role as a leader in world affairs.

The trouble is that America is run by human beings who struggle to understand and live up to these ideals. So our history describes numerous periods of social confrontation and self-examination that expose the ways we violate our own principles. The civil rights movement was one of those conflicts. The worst kind of oppression existed in this country just fifty years ago.

From the time of Reconstruction to the 1950s and early 1960s, it was very dangerous for black people simply to go to the courthouse and ask to register to vote. In places throughout the South—in Selma and Montgomery, Alabama; in Jackson and Philadelphia, Mississippi; in Albany and Atlanta, Georgia—people were run out of town. They lost their jobs and their farms. They were beaten, arrested, and even killed for sitting next to a white person at a lunch counter or on a public bus and for trying to register to vote.

There came a time when, as the great activist Fannie Lou Hamer once said, people got sick and tired of being sick and tired, and they began a movement that changed America forever. I was one of those people. We submitted to training in the discipline and philosophy of nonviolence, rooted in Christian faith, grounded in the history of Mahatma Gandhi's campaigns in India and Africa, and led by the greatest moral leader of our time, Reverend Martin Luther King, Jr.

We were just ordinary people, but we had extraordinary vision. We heard the voice of a higher calling that confirmed our inalienable rights.

We believed our humanity demanded respect. We believed that if we held to the discipline and philosophy of nonviolence and did not sway, then we could help build the Beloved Community in America, an all-encompassing society based on simple justice that values the dignity and the worth of every human being.

We didn't have a cell phone or a computer. We didn't have a website or even a fax machine, but we used what we had, and we had ourselves. We put our bodies on the line to bring down the system of legalized segregation and racial discrimination. So when the police and state troopers attacked us with bullwhips or billy clubs, when we were trampled by horses, chased by police dogs, or knocked down by fire hoses, we did not raise our hands to hit back.

We did not arm ourselves with guns, sticks, or knives. We armed ourselves with a dream. If our goal was peace and the brotherhood of humankind, then we believed we had to use peaceful means to achieve peaceful ends. We believed that since we are all one people, one human family, our nonviolent confrontation was an act of love meant to redeem the souls of our attackers and rescue a nation locked in the prison of violence.

Because of these ordinary people with extraordinary vision, this nation witnessed a nonviolent revolution under the rule of law, a revolution of values and ideas that transformed this nation forever. Today people of all races sit together at lunch counters and on buses across America. People can register to vote at the grocery store, at their churches, or in the comfort of their own homes. They do not have to risk their lives any more to go to the polls and select the candidate of their choice.

Today many are not aware, and others have the luxury to forget, that Americans gave their lives so they could exercise their freedom today. That is what is sacred about the places in this guide. This book is the commemoration of a legacy—a legacy of struggle and a legacy of liberation that keeps this nation evolving ever closer to its highest and most fulfilling destiny. It is a tribute to all the people who shed blood and even died for the cause of peace, the cause of justice, and the cause of equality in our society. It is a reminder that democracy is not a state; it is an act. And each generation must follow the call to do what is right, fair, and just to realize the fundamental principles of our founding. And finally, it is a testament that as citizens of this nation and members of a world society, we all have a mandate to do what we can to help build the Beloved Community, a nation and a world at peace with itself.

Honorable John Lewis
US Congressman
5th Congressional District, Georgia

Preface

The following guide identifies the major sites of civil rights actions in Atlanta from the 1940s to the present and provides details about the activities and individuals associated with the sites. However, the guide primarily focuses on what occurred between 1957 and 1968, when activists in Atlanta used direct action tactics to desegregate the Atlanta Public Library, the Atlanta Municipal Auditorium, the railroad and bus terminals, and a variety of downtown businesses, restaurants, hotels, churches, entertainment venues, and recreational establishments. The guide also highlights the activities of two of the most successful civil rights organizations in the 1950s and 1960s—the Southern Christian Leadership Conference (SCLC) and the Student Nonviolent Coordinating Committee (SNCC)—both of which had their headquarters in Atlanta during the 1960s. SCLC is still headquartered in Atlanta.

The activists used a variety of nonviolent methods to fight for social justice and human rights: sitting-in at restaurants and other public facilities, kneeling-in at segregated white churches, lying-in at Henry Grady Hotel, organizing a boycott at Rich's department store, singing protest and freedom songs, writing letters to the newspapers, and organizing conferences, marches, vigils, and picket lines. Many involved in these actions were arrested, fined, and incarcerated in the city's and county's prisons and jails.

There are four walking and driving tours detailed in the guide. The first three provide information about sites located within a single neighborhood or that lie along a specific street. Thus, visits to these sites could be organized as walking tours. If you choose to take walking tours, you should allow an hour and a half to two hours to complete each tour. The sites discussed in Tour 4 (Four Scattered Sites) are located in each of the four quadrants of the city. These sites can be visited most conveniently by car but can also be reached by public transportation. For details about specific sites in the four tours, see the section of the guide devoted to each tour. For information about the location of the sites and how to reach the sites by car or MARTA (Metropolitan Atlanta Rapid Transit Authority), see the directions and maps at the beginning of each tour as well as the index of sites with GPS coordinates in the back of the book.

Representatives from Atlanta's political, business, civic, and educational communities are making plans to build a Center for Civil and Human Rights (CCHR) in downtown Atlanta. The center will highlight the pre-twentieth-century worldwide efforts to achieve civil and human rights, as well as the contributions of Atlantans and Georgians to the struggles for civil and human rights in the twentieth and twenty-first centuries. The center also will provide opportunities for ongoing dialogue and study of ways to resolve current civil and human rights abuses in Atlanta and around the world.

After the center is open in 2010, a visit to the facility would be an ideal way to begin and/or end the tours described in this guide. **(FOR MORE DETAILS ABOUT THE CENTER, SEE THE SECTION, "CENTER FOR CIVIL AND HUMAN RIGHTS.")**

The two authors contributed to the development of the guide in the following ways: Lefever wrote the text, some of which he adapted from his book, Undaunted By The Fight: Spelman College and the Civil Rights Movement, 1957–1967.[1] Also, unless otherwise acknowledged, Lefever took the photographs. Page constructed the maps and the index of sites with GPS coordinates. Both authors collaborated on the design of the tours and the guide.

For updates to the guide and downloadable GPS coordinates, visit the Sacred Places website at www.waypoints.net/sacredplaces/.

Finally, a few words of explanation about the title of the guide: we chose the title Sacred Places because we are aware that these sites represent people and events that evoke strong emotions in many visitors. These places evoke, both consciously and unconsciously, the ultimate concerns that motivate religious behavior. As with the visitors to other historical sites such as the Lincoln Memorial and the Vietnam Memorial in Washington, visitors to the civil rights sites in Atlanta often express "religious" attitudes and behavior such as silence and hushed tones.

For those who initially are not aware of the sacredness of the places they are visiting, we hope that this guide will help them experience the people, events, and symbols associated with these sites with the deep respect and reverence they deserve.

Brief History of the Civil Rights Movement in Atlanta

(In the 1950s and 1960s)

On January 1, 1957, less than a month after the conclusion of the successful bus boycott led by Martin Luther King, Jr., in Montgomery, Alabama, the Atlanta chapter of the NAACP organized an afternoon rally at the Big Bethel AME Church on Auburn Avenue to discuss the ending of segregation practices in Atlanta. The group in attendance packed the sanctuary and spilled over into the corridors, the basement, and the sidewalks outside the church. After the reading of the Fourteenth Amendment and excerpts from the Emancipation Proclamation, Martin Luther King, Jr., who had come from Montgomery for the meeting, spoke. During his speech, King referred to the Montgomery Bus Boycott and how the Negro citizens there "walked in pride rather than ride in humiliation" and stressed that the same could happen in Atlanta. He said it was important that the Negro race stick together and stand up for their rights as given them by the Constitution of the United States.

A few days later, more than one hundred of Atlanta's African-American ministers engaged in an attempt to desegregate Atlanta's trolleys and buses. Rather than organize a bus boycott as had occurred in Montgomery, their organization, called the Triple L Movement (Law, Love, and Liberation), planned to establish a test case that would challenge the segregated seating patterns on Georgia's trolleys and buses.

On January 9, more than thirty black ministers, including Martin Luther King, Sr., pastor of Ebenezer Baptist Church, and William Holmes Borders, pastor of Wheat Street Baptist Church, boarded a local bus and sat in various sections, including vacant front seats. None of the participants was arrested. That evening Borders organized a rally at his church on Auburn Avenue. He spoke about the day's events with the more than 700 in attendance and promised that the ministers would repeat their "sit-down" action the next day. He assured the enthusiastic crowd that they would continue their actions until the trolleys and buses were desegregated, saying, "This crusade for freedom will not stop. We're going to ride these buses desegregated in Atlanta, Georgia, or we're going to ride a chariot in heaven or push a wheelbarrow in hell."[2]

The next day, six ministers, including Rev. Borders, boarded a bus and sat on the front seats. This time they were arrested and taken to the police station in a paddy wagon. Ironically, the paddy wagon was driven by a Negro policeman. (The first Negro policemen were hired in Atlanta in 1948.)

At the police station the ministers were fingerprinted, questioned, charged, and released on a $1000 bond each. On January 15, a Fulton County grand jury indicted the six ministers on charges of ignoring the state's segregation laws. If convicted, the

Ministers sitting in jail. Rev. William Holmes Borders in on the far right.

six could have been sentenced to twelve months in a public works camp or a $1000 fine and six months in a camp. However, they were never tried. More than two years after their indictment, a federal court declared segregated seating on Atlanta's trolleys and buses to be unconstitutional.

During the same month that the black ministers were involved in their efforts to desegregate Atlanta's trolleys and buses, a group of Atlanta University Center (AUC) students active in Spelman's Social Science Club made a visit to the Georgia Legislature assembled in the capitol downtown. (At the time the Atlanta University Center included the following six institutions: Spelman College, Morehouse College, Clark College, Morris Brown College, Atlanta University, and the Interdenominational Theological Center [ITC].) **(SEE TOUR 2 FOR DETAILS ON THE ATLANTA UNIVERSITY CENTER INSTITUTIONS.)** The original purpose of the visit was merely to observe the legislative proceedings. However, when the students and their advisor, Spelman history professor Howard Zinn, arrived and saw the gallery separated into "white" and "Negro" sections, they quickly decided to ignore the signs and sit in the "white" section. Later, Zinn reported that when the speaker of the house, Marvin E. Moate, saw the students sitting in the "white" section, he (the speaker) developed "a quick case of apoplexy and rushed to the microphone to shout: 'You nigras move over to where you belong! We got segregation in the state of Georgia!'" Zinn said that after a brief consultation, he and the students decided to watch the proceedings from the "colored" section of the gallery.[3]

A year later, Zinn and a group of students returned to the legislature. This time they decided to protest silently by standing in the "white" section of the gallery. The speaker again demanded that the group leave. Zinn and the students filed out through the nearest door "to the accompaniment of loud applause from the legislators." However, before the applause had died down, the group reentered through another door and "stood near the colored section, maintaining their resolve not to sit down in a segregated section." The gallery remained segregated for another five years. Finally, in January 1963, it was desegregated along with other state facilities. When the day of desegregation finally came, Zinn and a group of students were there to mark the occasion.[4]

In the spring of 1959, a group of Spelman and Morehouse students and faculty organized actions to desegregate the Atlanta Public Library. They visited the central facility downtown, selected books and other materials, and then attempted to borrow the items at the checkout desk. Their requests were denied. At the same time, the Atlanta Council on Human Relations, an interracial group, lobbied the library board of trustees to open the library system to everyone.

When these tactics of gentle pressure failed, Howard Zinn and Whitney Young, dean of the School of Social Work at Atlanta University, began to prepare a federal lawsuit against the library. Two willing plaintiffs stepped forward—Rev. Otis Moss, Jr., a Morehouse theology student, and Dr. Irene Dobbs Jackson, a 1929 Spelman alumna who, at the time, was teaching French at Spelman.

On Tuesday, May 19, as Zinn was in Young's office discussing the lawsuit, a member of the library's board of trustees called and announced to Young that the board had decided to integrate the library system—but it requested that the integration be delayed a few days so that the director of the library system could inform his staff about the change. Young and Zinn agreed to give them until Friday.

Carnegie Library. In 1980 this Beaux Arts structure was torn down and replaced with the current building.

On Friday afternoon, May 22, Irene Jackson walked into the Carnegie Library, went to the front desk and applied for and received a library card. She was the first black so honored. Earl A. Sanders, a Spelman music professor, also received his card at the same time. Within days, two Spelman students and a Morehouse student were issued their cards.

In 1983, in a return visit to Spelman, Jackson related the story of her involvement in the integration of the library. She told her audience that she still carried the library card she had received in 1959. The card, she declared, was "a glowing, though time-worn symbol of the right to the liberty of knowledge [and] an extension of our right to education."[5]

On February 1, 1960, Martin Luther King, Jr., and his family moved from Montgomery, Alabama, to Atlanta. King became co-pastor with his father at Ebenezer Baptist Church on Auburn Avenue and continued his duties as president of the Southern Christian Leadership Conference (SCLC) at the organization's office a few blocks from the church. **(SEE TOUR 1 FOR DETAILS ABOUT AUBURN AVENUE.)**

The date of the King family move to Atlanta coincided with another significant event in civil rights history. February 1, 1960, is generally recognized as the beginning of the sit-in phase of the civil rights movement. That was the day when four black students from North Carolina A & T College in Greensboro sat down at a "white-only" lunch counter in the local Woolworth's department store. The four students were refused service. The incident made national headlines, and the sit-in movement was launched.

Two or three days later, a group of Atlanta University Center students were relaxing in the Yates and Milton Drugstore at the corner of Fair

Irene Jackson speaking at Spelman.

and Chestnut (now Brawley) Streets in southwest Atlanta.

Among the students were two Morehouse College men—Lonnie King and Julian Bond. Lonnie was reading a newspaper story about the Greensboro sit-it. He walked over to Julian and asked him if he had seen the story. The two talked about what was happening in Greensboro and decided to convene a meeting that afternoon in Sale Hall on the Morehouse campus to discuss organizing demonstrations in Atlanta. Twelve students showed up. As attendance increased over the next few days, they held a series of workshops on how to carry out protest demonstrations nonviolently.

Yates & Milton Drug Store

When the council of presidents of the Atlanta University Center heard about the students' plans, they asked to meet with them. During late February and early March the students and presidents met several times. At one of the meetings, President Rufus Clement from Atlanta University suggested that the students write a statement about their grievances. The students accepted the challenge.

On March 9, 1960, the statement was published as a full-page ad in Atlanta's three major newspapers—the Atlanta Constitution, the Atlanta Journal, and the Atlanta Daily World. In the statement, titled "An Appeal for Human Rights," the students declared that they would not "sit by submissively, while being denied all the rights, privileges, and joys of life."

They also provided details about the inequities and injustices existing in Atlanta and throughout Georgia in seven areas of public and private life—education; jobs; housing; voting; hospitals; movies, concerts, and restaurants; and law enforcement—and called for radical changes. The statement was signed by a student representative from each of the six institutions in the Atlanta University Center.

An Appeal for Human Rights

We, the students of the six affiliated institutions forming the Atlanta University Center…have joined our hearts, minds, and bodies in the cause of gaining those rights, which are inherently ours as members of the human race and as citizens of the United States.…

We do not intend to wait placidly for those rights, which are already legally and morally ours to be meted out to us one at a time. Today's youth will not sit by submissively, while being denied all of the rights, privileges, and joys of life. We want to state clearly and unequivocally that we cannot tolerate, in a nation professing democracy and among people professing Christianity, the discriminatory conditions under which the Negro is living today in Atlanta, Georgia—supposedly one of the most progressive cities in the South.…

We, therefore, call upon all people in authority— State, County, and City officials, all leaders in civic life—ministers, teachers, business men, and all people of good will to assert themselves and abolish these injustices. We must say in all candor that we plan to use every legal and non-violent means at our disposal to secure full citizenship rights as members of this great Democracy of ours.

The manifesto received much local and national attention. Responses ranged from negative to moderate to positive. Georgia governor Ernest Vandiver was extremely critical and sarcastic in his response:

> *I have read the "paid advertisement" purporting to come from students of the six affiliated institutions forming the Atlanta University Center. The statement was skillfully prepared. Obviously, it was not written by students. Regrettably, it had the same overtones which are usually found in anti-American propaganda pieces. It did not sound like it was prepared in any Georgia school or college; nor, in fact, did it read like it was written even in this country. This left-wing statement is calculated to breed dissatisfaction, discontent, discord and evil.*[6]

The response from Mayor William B. Hartsfield was cautiously supportive, saying that the manifesto was "of the greatest importance to the City of Atlanta" and that it expressed "the legitimate aspirations of young people throughout the nation and the entire world." In addition, he lauded the students for their promise of a nonviolent and peaceful approach.[7]

On the afternoon of March 10, one day after the manifesto was published, a small group of AUC students and faculty gathered on Spelman's campus with plans to attend a matinee performance of My Fair Lady at the Municipal Auditorium (30 Courtland Avenue; now Georgia State University's Alumni Hall). Henry West, a young white philosophy professor at Spelman, had purchased tickets for the six individuals in the group. The tickets were for

Municipal Auditorium

the "white" orchestra section, the best seats in
the house.

When the six arrived at the Municipal
Auditorium, the attendant took their tickets and
returned the stubs before he realized what was
happening. Flustered, he mumbled "wait a moment,
please" and ran for the manager. The group, holding
their stubs, decided not to wait. A "slightly bewil-
dered usher" conducted them to their seats. Within
moments the manager appeared and asked them to
move. They refused. He pleaded, "Why don't you
leave and we'll return your money. You know, if you
don't leave all of these people will be deprived of
seeing the show." When the group remained in their
seats, the manager rushed to his office and called
Mayor Hartsfield. The mayor thought a moment
and then said, "The only suggestion I can make is
that you dim the lights." The manager immediately
declared the seats where the six were sitting a Negro
section, thus making the seating "legal."

Inspired by the widespread attention that their
manifesto had generated, a group of AUC students

had their first sit-in on March 15. Approximately two hundred students from across the Center participated. By the end of the day, seventy-seven students were arrested. In addition, the six students who signed the manifesto were also arrested. All eighty-three were charged with breaching the peace, intimidating restaurant owners, refusing to leave the premises, and conspiracy. Fortunately, they were never tried.

April 10, 1960, was Spelman's eighty-ninth Founders' Day Celebration. The speaker for the occasion was Martin Luther King, Jr., who, in his remarks, made reference to the developing student movement: "Segregation is a cancer in the body politic which must be removed before our democratic health can be realized.... This is why the student movement...all over our country is so significant.... The beautiful thing...is that you are not merely demanding service at the lunch counter...you're not merely demanding a cup of coffee and a hamburger.... You are demanding respect."[8]

On May 17, 1960, the sixth anniversary of the Brown v. Board of Education Supreme Court decision, several thousand AUC students marched to the state capitol. However, police barred them from the capitol grounds, so the students diverted their march to the Wheat Street Baptist Church where they held a rally. Later that evening, they organized an entertaining fund-raiser known as "Sit-in Showdown" at Davage Auditorium at Clark College.

Following the commencement exercises in May, most of the students enrolled in the six Atlanta University Center schools returned home for the summer or left the city for other summer activities. However, a handful remained in Atlanta and continued to plan for and engage in movement activities. Aware of the importance of the support of the black community for the success of their efforts, the students developed a program called "The Student Movement and You," which they presented through the summer to various black churches and civic groups. In addition, they persuaded two radio stations to carry weekly news shows on the student movement, and published a weekly mimeographed newsletter called "The Student Movement and You."

Along with their efforts to increase community support, the students organized several sit-ins at Rich's department store downtown. Targeted were

JULY 31, 1960

The Student Movement And
YOU

The struggle of the **Negro** in Atlanta for **FULL RIGHTS** is underway.

NO NEGRO WITH THE INTEREST OF HIS PEOPLE AT HEART CAN SHOP IN THOSE STORES NOW BEING BOYCOTTED.

Negro buying power can make the difference between profit and loss for businesses. **WE MUST NOT** CONTINUE TO USE THIS BUYING POWER TO MAKE SEGREGATION PROFITABLE.

NOW IS THE TIME FOR ATLANTANS TO **ACT!** CLOSE YOUR ACCOUNT WITH SEGREGATION.

Issued by:
COMMITTEE ON APPEAL FOR HUMAN RIGHTS
Paid Advertisement

The Student Movement and You advertisement[9]

The Bridge, the Barbecue Room and the Cockerel Grill, all popular eating places at Rich's. When the owners failed to change their segregated policies, the students called for a boycott of the store. Aware that Rich's was the flagship of Atlanta's department stores, the students believed that if they caused Rich's to lose money, the other department stores would take note. The students contacted many in the black community and argued that it was unjust for black patrons who spent thousands of dollars at Rich's to be forced to use a dirty basement restroom and drink at the "colored" water fountain. Those who refused to support the boycott were "working against all Negroes who want equality, dignity, and full opportunity."[10] The students chose a slogan to publicize the boycott: "Close out your charge account with segregation; open up your account with freedom."

Many black customers responded by sending in their charge cards or closing their accounts. One man who closed his account was John Wesley Dobbs. In a letter to Rich's management, Dobbs stated that he was closing his account because, in spite of his numerous appeals and protests, nothing had changed at the store. He stated that he and the Reverend Martin Luther King, Sr., had talked with Mr. Rich personally about the injustices at the store, but their efforts were "to no avail." Mr. Dobbs wrote, "We have sent Committees to see you, we have written letters of protest, but none of these appeals have [sic] caused you to change your attitude and policy toward your Colored Patrons.... Your policy of 'JIM-CROW' treatment to your Colored Patrons is positively WRONG, and UNFAIR. You are caught on the wrong side of a MORAL ISSUE."[11]

In August 1960, the students organized a series of "kneel-ins" at white churches. On August 7, twenty-five students sat in at six white churches—First Baptist, Druid Hills Baptist, First Presbyterian, St. Mark's Methodist, Grace Methodist, and the Episcopal Cathedral of St. Philip. Only two of the six, First Presbyterian and the Episcopal Cathedral of St. Philip, allowed the students to sit with the congregation. All the others either refused them entrance or required that they stand or sit in the lobby.

On the following Sunday, August 14, the students organized another kneel-in. They were accepted at five churches—First Presbyterian, St. Luke's Episcopal, Central Presbyterian, Lutheran Church of the Redeemer, and Second Ponce de Leon Baptist— but were turned away at Grace Methodist, Druid Hills Baptist, Baptist Tabernacle, Druid Hills Methodist, and First Baptist (where they had to view the service from an adjoining room).

Early in the 1960 school term, students from across the Atlanta University Center planned sit-ins for October 19 at eight downtown department stores. The eight businesses targeted were Rich's, S. H. Kress, F. W. Woolworth, H. L. Green, Newberry's, Grant's, and McCrory's. Rich's, however, was the primary target. On October 18, Herschelle Sullivan from Spelman and Lonnie King from Morehouse (co-chairs of the student organization, the Committee On Appeal for Human Rights [COAHR]) called Martin Luther King, Jr., and invited him to join the students in demonstrations planned for the next day. Lonnie later recalled that at first King was reluctant to join the students because he was on probation in DeKalb County for failing to change his drivers license when he moved from Montgomery to Atlanta. If arrested again, King said, he would be in violation of his probation. Lonnie reminded King that he was the spiritual leader of the movement and that he would "add tremendous impetus" to the students' actions. King reluctantly agreed to join them.[12]

As promised, the following morning King joined the students at Rich's. Shortly after his arrival, he and a group of students were arrested at Rich's elegant Magnolia Tea Room on the sixth floor. By the end of the day, fifty-one students were arrested at a variety of downtown restaurants. As King had predicted, DeKalb County judge Oscar Mitchell revoked his probation. Showing no mercy, Judge Mitchell ordered King to serve four months at hard labor on a road gang at the state prison in Reidsville.

The demonstration and King's arrest occurred two weeks before the November 1960 presidential election. The candidates were John Kennedy and Richard Nixon. When Senator Kennedy heard about King's incarceration, he called Mrs. King to express his concern. A short time later Robert Kennedy called the judge. The next day King was released. Kennedy later said he told the judge that if he were a decent American, he would let King out by sundown, adding, "It made me so damn angry to think of that bastard sentencing a citizen to four months of hard labor for a minor traffic offense."[13]

On November 8, in one of the closest presidential elections in US history, Kennedy beat Nixon by less than two-tenths of one percent of the popular vote. When blacks had heard of the Kennedys' intervention in King's release, many decided to vote for Kennedy. This last minute support put Kennedy over the top.

On February 7, 1961, a group of AUC students was arrested for a sit-in at Sprayberry's Cafeteria on Peachtree Street. Over the next two days, dozens more were arrested at Sprayberry's and other restaurants. All were incarcerated in the Fulton County Jail, or, as the students called it, the "Hilton Bars." The seventy-two incarcerated students created an acute housing problem at the jail; the jailer reported that he had only three beds—but plenty of floor space—left.

On May 17, 1961, four leaders of COAHR—Herschelle Sullivan from Spelman, Lonnie King and Charles Lyles from Morehouse, and Benjamin Brown from Clark—filed a federal law suit citing discrimination in all city-owned facilities such as parks, swimming pools, tennis courts, the municipal auditorium, and the municipal courts. The students, acting without the aid of an attorney, choose to file the suit on May 17, the seventh anniversary of the Brown v. Board of Education decision outlawing segregation in the public schools.

The four students filed their suit as a class action on behalf of all 230,000 black Atlanta residents. In their suit they stated that "the ten-thousand-and-one instances (which occur daily) of total exclusion because of race or segregation by race in the use and enjoyment of the facilities of the City of Atlanta [are] done...under color of law and based solely on race." Such practices, the students declared, "are insulting, degrading, unnecessary, medieval, foolish, septic and unconstitutional."[14]

The following day the Atlanta Constitution editors praised the students for moving their activity from the streets to the courts: "These matters [of desegregation] are best committed to the orderly processes of the courts [rather] than to displays in the streets.... The students have shown a sense of their own responsibility for proceeding with their activities in the interest of community calm."[15]

Fifteen months later, on August 27, 1962, the federal court ruled in the students' favor. Benjamin Brown declared the decision a "tremendous victory for the Committee On Appeal For Human Rights, who so untiringly manifested their concern for the malpractices on the part of public officials in perpetuating racial discrimination."[16] Howard Zinn, professor of history and chair of the Social Science Department at Spelman, likewise praised the ruling: "It was the most sweeping legal victory for civil rights in Atlanta's history, and four students had done it on their own."[17]

In June 1962, Spelman student Ruby Doris Smith and seven other plaintiffs filed a federal lawsuit against Henry Grady Hospital in downtown Atlanta, charging that the hospital practiced racial discrimination and segregation.[18] The suit was brought on behalf of Ruby Doris, who had applied for admission to the Grady Hospital nursing school and had been rejected because of her race. The suit challenged the racial discrimination and segregation in the hospital's classrooms and living facilities and asked for the desegregation of all segregated patient-care facilities, staff facilities, and student training programs at Grady. It also demanded the desegregation of local and state medical societies. The suit failed. Ruby Doris was not admitted to the nursing school, and the segregated practices continued.

Six months after the failed Grady Hospital suit, one of its plaintiffs, Spelman College physician Dr. Clinton E. Warner, became embroiled in another civil rights contest. This time his action was directed at Atlanta's segregated housing patterns.

In December 1962, Dr. Warner purchased a house in Peyton Forest, an exclusive white neighborhood in southwest Atlanta. When the purchase became

The "Atlanta Wall"

known, a group of white neighbors rushed to city hall to demand that their neighborhood's segregation be preserved. Following their visit, the board of aldermen's public works committee conferred with Mayor Ivan Allen, Jr. Together they devised a plan to erect a number of barricades in an effort to prevent blacks from entering the neighborhood. The board of aldermen voted approval for the plan on the afternoon of December 17. At seven o'clock the following morning, city work crews appeared in Peyton Forest and began erecting nearly three-foot-high wood and steel barricades across Peyton and Harlan Roads, the only two streets running north and south through the neighborhood.

The barricades remained until March 1, 1963, when a Superior Court judge, George P. Whitman, in response to a lawsuit, ruled that the barricades were unconstitutional and ordered their immediate removal. (SEE TOUR 4 FOR MORE DETAILS ABOUT THE "ATLANTA WALL.")

On the morning of March 13, 1963, five Atlanta University Center students—one white and four black—appeared at Henry Grady Hotel in downtown Atlanta with confirmed mail reservations for that evening. The white student was Anna Jo Weaver, an exchange student at Spelman; the four black students were Gwendolyn Iles, a Spelman senior; Willie P. Berrien from Clark; and Amos Brown and Timothy Wilson from Morehouse. Anna Jo, who had made the reservations for the group, entered the hotel ahead of the other four and was immediately assigned a room. However, when the four black students arrived a short time later, they were denied accommodations.

As planned, those denied accommodations moved to the lobby where they staged a "lie-in." They opened their suitcases, removed pillows and blankets, and made themselves comfortable on the sofas in the hotel lobby. Two weeks later, Jet magazine published a picture of Gwendolyn lying on a sofa covered with a blanket and a male guest seated nearby. Under the picture was the caption: "A guest at Grady calmly surveys a Spelman College student who reads 'Politics Among Nations' while lying-in in hotel lobby."[19] Policemen were called and the students were ordered to leave. Gwendolyn complied, but Willie and Amos refused and were arrested.

The day following the "lie-in," several hundred Atlanta University Center students marched from Grady Hotel to city hall. The group, led by the co-chairs of COAHR, Gwendolyn Iles from Spelman and Ralph Moore from Morehouse, gathered on the steps of city hall and sang until Mayor Ivan Allen, Jr., appeared. When he arrived, Gwendolyn read the following letter:

We the members of the Committee on Appeal for Human Rights, representing the six affiliated institutions of the Atlanta University Center, are very dissatisfied with the situation regarding desegregation in our metropolitan city....

We are confronting you with this problem because we feel that you, as Mayor, can exert more influence upon the situation than you have in the past. We ask that your office take action immediately regarding the breaking down of racial barriers, not only in the hotels but in every area where racial segregation exists....

We call upon you to move immediately to eradicate these evils which have stymied Atlanta's progress.

We must say in all candor that we plan to use every legal and non-violent means at our disposal to secure full citizenship rights as members of this great Democracy of ours.[20]

Mayor Allen listened patiently as Gwendolyn read the letter. Then he told the students that the city always has had "the courage to face up to its problems." He added that the students "could save shoe leather" by not marching on city hall but by simply inviting him to go out to their colleges and "discuss anything" with him.[21]

Among the students arrested in the many lunch-counter demonstrations in early January 1964 were Spelman students Mardon Walker and Gwendolyn Robinson. Mardon, a white exchange student from the Connecticut College for Women, was among sixteen students arrested at two Krystal restaurants in downtown Atlanta on January 13. Following her arrest, she was taken to the Fulton Superior Court where Judge Durwood Pye scheduled a trial for

February 19. In spite of positive testimony from her Spelman professor, Melvin Drimmer, the jury convicted her of violating Georgia's anti-trespass law (refusing to leave a privately operated eating establishment when requested to do so). Following the jury's conviction, Judge Pye gave her the maximum sentence for a misdemeanor offense—six months in jail, twelve months on the public works, and a $1,000 fine.

Following her conviction and before she was freed on bond, Mardon spent several days in the Fulton County Jail. A sympathetic white woman, Nan Pendergrast, read about Mardon's incarceration and sent her a letter of support. In her two-page reply to Mrs. Pendergrast, Mardon explained her feelings about her arrest: "Being here is humiliating in a sense—one loses one's dignity so easily in such a situation—but the tragedy is not in my being here, but rather that the Negroes in our country feel the same loss of dignity, the same humiliation every day of their lives…. Freedom is such a general, sometimes trite-sounding phrase but it really means something to me…. I wish white people could understand that when the Negro Youth cries 'FREEDOM, NOW!' he is speaking not just of freedom for the Negro, but freedom for the white also."[22]

Mardon was released on February 22 when two Atlantans paid her $15,000 bond. She returned home to East Greenwich, Rhode Island, took a year off from college to work with disadvantaged kids in New Haven, and then completed the requirements for graduation at Connecticut College for Women.

Mardon appealed her conviction to the Georgia Supreme Court, which, on November 5, 1964, ruled to uphold her conviction. She then appealed to the US Supreme Court, which, more than six months later, on May 24, 1965, in a 5–4 vote, reversed the Georgia Supreme Court's decision and voided her conviction.

Gwendolyn Robinson enrolled at Spelman in the fall of 1962 and gradually became involved in civil rights activities. At first, she offered her services as a volunteer in the SNCC office a few blocks from Spelman, but by the spring of 1964, she was deeply involved in direct action demonstrations. Although she had promised herself and her grandmother that she would not get arrested, she was arrested while picketing at Lester Maddox's Pickrick Restaurant. She and several fellow students spent one night in jail. **(SEE TOUR 4 FOR A PHOTOGRAPH OF THE PICKRICK RESTAURANT AND MORE DETAILS ON LESTER MADDOX.)**

When Gwen and the others returned to the campus the following day, they knew they were in trouble. As expected, the dean of students called Gwen into her office where she was questioned about leaving campus without permission, lying on the dorm sign-out sheet, and disobeying Spelman's regulations prohibiting participation in civil rights demonstrations. She was put on probation.

However, Gwen was not deterred. A few days later she and fellow students entered one of the targeted restaurants and asked for a cup of coffee and a hamburger. When told the restaurant was closed, the group refused to leave and were attacked by a group of white men. Police soon arrived and arrested the students.

Gwendolyn Robinson's
Report of a 1964 Sit-in

All of a sudden several young white men came running in from the back of the establishment with sticks and clubs in their hands.... Before I could think, I...jumped across the counter trying to get away from one of the male attackers, only to be jumped by one of the waitresses.... I then began throwing cups, saucers and dishes at the attackers trying to keep them off of me.... The place was in a shambles and a bloody row was in progress when "Atlanta's Finest" came, stopped the fracas and arrested all [the students].[23]

Gwen and her friends spent the next three days in jail. Having violated her probation, Gwen knew that she was now in serious trouble at Spelman. When she returned to campus, President Manley called her into his office and asked if she were a communist and if she had been sent "to foment dissent and chaos on the campus"? The dean of students then informed her that her scholarship had been revoked and that she'd better start packing her suitcase.

Word of Gwen's dismissal quickly spread across campus and through the Atlanta University Center. Within hours, friends and fellow demonstrators began planning a protest march and demonstration. The next day, during the lunch period, more than one hundred students and SNCC workers marched to President Manley's house on campus and held a rally. Some declared they would organize a boycott of classes. Somehow, the protests worked. Gwen was permitted to remain at Spelman for the remainder of the semester under strict probation.

During the last week of January 1964, hundreds of demonstrators turned their attention to several Leb's

restaurants downtown. On the first day, as demonstrators picketed in front of the restaurant, they were
joined by a group of hooded Klansmen led by an old
man dressed in the white satin costume of a Klan
Cyclops. Following close behind were a number of
white-robed individuals and a half-dozen white boys
and men. The police watched with apprehension as
the white line moved through the narrow space in
front of the demonstrators on the sidewalk. The
demonstrators, holding their ground, responded with
rousing renditions of "The old K-K, she ain't what
she used to be" and "We Shall Overcome."

Walking with the picketers was the comedian Dick
Gregory, who, accompanied by his pregnant wife,
Lillian, had come to Atlanta to participate in the
protests. As he walked, Gregory listened with delight
to the call-and-response refrains emanating from the
picket line. At the same time, he was distracted by
the Klansman, draped in the Cyclops costume and
parading across the street. Fascinated by the dramatic
nature of the scene, Gregory crossed the street,
walked up to Cyclops, looked him straight in the
eye, and in as reverent a tone as his comedic self
would allow asked, "Is that you, Lawd?"

An additional contingent of Klansmen soon
arrived to join the marching hooded men. Several
black demonstrators, their heads draped with white
tablecloths "borrowed" from Leb's, mockingly fell in
step behind the Klansmen. After hours of singing
and dramatic performances on both sides of the
street, the police ordered the black protesters to
leave. When they refused, many, including Dick
Gregory, were arrested for disorderly conduct and
disturbing the peace.[24]

Also arrested was Gloria Bishop, an instructor of
English at Spelman.[25] Bishop was arrested on

January 27 and spent almost five days in jail. According to Bishop, the beds were covered with "bug-infested mattresses and filthy blue sheets" and their only choice was to use "seatless, unclean, and tissueless" toilets. Bishop's jail mates were alcoholics, vagrants, prostitutes, shoplifters, and women who had used weapons to defend themselves against abusive husbands or lovers. The demonstrators spent many hours listening to the other prisoners talk about their problems. According to Bishop, "we were the dreamers, the messengers of hope, the healing hands who could make a difference in the world and therefore a difference in their lives. We were like royalty in a place where there were no thrones."[26]

Bishop and the other demonstrators were released at 2:30 A.M. on their fifth day of incarceration. As she walked through the stockade door, Bishop gratefully embraced her freedom: "What a relief that the door was shutting us, not inside as before, but outside where the air was free from the odor of urine and the smell of too-obvious inhumanity. And so, twenty-five hours after entering the stockade and four and a half days after being arrested, I was once again free—to the extent that Negroes are in this country and in this city 'too busy to hate.'"[27]

On December 10, 1964, Martin Luther King, Jr., received the Nobel Peace Prize in Oslo, Norway. In his acceptance speech, King said that the Prize symbolized his abiding faith in America and the future of mankind: "I refuse to accept the view that mankind is so tragically bound to the starless midnight of racism and war that the bright daybreak of peace and brotherhood can never become a reality.… When our days become dreary with low-hovering clouds and our nights become darker than a thousand midnights, we will know that we are living in the creative turmoil of a genuine civilization struggling to be born."[28]

Six weeks later, on January 27, 1965, King was honored at an integrated dinner at the Dinkler Hotel in downtown Atlanta. Life magazine declared that "it would have been a memorable moment in any US city when 1,500 leading citizens, black and white alike, stood after dinner to sing We Shall Overcome." But, the Life journalist continued, the event was "doubly memorable" because the city was Atlanta and the guest of honor was Dr. Martin Luther King, Jr."[29]

43

Nobel Peace Prize Dinner
Honoring Martin Luther King, Jr.

Greetings by Rabbi Jacob Rothschild
The National Anthem
The Invocation by Rev. Samuel Williams
Introduction of Dais Guests
Dinner
Music by Morehouse College Choir
Tributes
Mayor Ivan Allen, Jr.
Bishop Ernest L. Hickman
Rev. Edward A. Driscoll
Senator Leroy Johnson
Archbishop Paul J. Hallinan
Introduction of Honoree by Dr. Benjamin E. Mays
Address—Dr. Martin Luther King, Jr.
Presentation of Gift
Benediction by Rev. Ralph Abernathy

The Nobel Peace Prize dinner, which should have been an occasion of pride and honor for all Atlantans, took place in an atmosphere of considerable resistance and controversy. Some bankers and businessmen criticized the dinner and threatened to boycott it. The Ku Klux Klan threatened to picket the hotel. A handful of city leaders, however, was supportive, including Ralph McGill, publisher of the Atlanta Constitution; Rabbi Jacob Rothschild, rabbi of The Temple, Atlanta's oldest and most prominent synagogue; Catholic archbishop Paul Hallinan; former mayor William B. Hartsfield; and the then-current mayor, Ivan Allen, Jr. McGill, Rothschild and Hallinan, along with Benjamin Mays, president of Morehouse College, co-chaired the preparations committee.

Following the dinner, Mayor Allen addressed the audience and honored King with the following words: "Through the years, as history is brought, some men are destined to be leaders of humanity and to shape the future course of the world. Dr. Martin Luther King, Jr., is such a man. I take great pride in honoring this citizen of Atlanta who is willing to turn the other cheek in his quest for full citizenship for all Americans."[30]

In May 1966, one year after her graduation from Spelman, Ruby Doris Smith Robinson was elected executive secretary of SNCC, the only woman ever to hold that position. She replaced Jim Forman. At the same time, Stokely Carmichael replaced John Lewis as chair.

Ruby Doris's tenure as SNCC executive secretary was tragically short. In January 1967, while in New York City to attend a SNCC fund-raising event, she became ill and was admitted to Beth Israel Hospital. After a series of tests, she was diagnosed with terminal cancer. In June, Ruby Doris was transferred from New York to Grady Hospital in Atlanta. However, the doctors at Grady soon concluded that there was little they could do for her and discharged her into the care of her family. She died at home on October 7, 1967. She was twenty-five years old. Survivors included her husband, Clifford; their two-year-old son, Kenneth Toure; her parents; and four brothers and two sisters. She is buried in South-View Cemetery in south Atlanta. **(SEE TOUR 4 FOR PHOTOGRAPHS OF RUBY DORIS AND HER GRAVESTONE AND FOR MORE DETAILS ABOUT HER CIVIL RIGHTS ACTIVITIES.)**

In many ways, Ruby Doris's death symbolized the end of the most creative years of the civil rights movement in Atlanta and elsewhere. Only six months after her death, on April 4, 1968, Martin Luther King, Jr., was assassinated in Memphis, Tennessee, while helping to organize the city's garbage workers. And, within a year of her death, the bankrupt SNCC was torn apart by political infighting. By 1970, SNCC ceased functioning as a viable organization.

Center for Civil and Human Rights

Corner of Centennial Olympic Park Dr.
and Ivan Allen, Jr. Blvd.
(next to the World of Coca-Cola Museum)
www.cchrpartnership.org

DIRECTIONS BY CAR FROM THE NORTH Take I-75/85 south to Williams Street (Exit 249C). At the end of the exit ramp, turn right on Ivan Allen, Jr. Blvd. The center will be immediately on your left.

DIRECTIONS BY CAR FROM THE SOUTH Take I-75-85 north to Spring Street/West Peachtree Street (Exit 249D). Turn right on Spring Street Ramp toward Centennial Olympic Park Dr. and bear right. Take an immediate left on to Ivan Allen, Jr. Blvd. The center will be immediately on your left.

DIRECTIONS BY MARTA Take the north/south line to the Civic Center Station (N2). Exit the station and walk south on West Peachtree Street. Turn right on Ivan Allen, Jr. Blvd. The center will be on the left after walking across Centennial Olympic Park Drive.

Representatives from Atlanta's political, business, civic, and educational communities are making plans to build a Center for Civil and Human Rights (CCHR,) in downtown Atlanta. A task force appointed by Atlanta mayor Shirley Franklin recommended that the center highlight three themes: (1) the worldwide underpinnings (from pre-history to the twentieth century) of civil and human rights philosophies and events leading up to the American civil rights movement; (2) the contributions of Atlantans and Georgians to the struggles for civil and human rights during slavery, the 1906 Atlanta race riot, and the 1950s–1960s civil rights movement; and (3) the ongoing dialogue and study of ways to resolve current and future struggles for civil and human rights in Atlanta and around the world.

A centerpiece of the CCHR will be an exhibit of some of the more than 7,000 notes, speeches, sermons, and other documents of Martin Luther King, Jr., that Morehouse College, in cooperation with Mayor Franklin and other civic, educational, and business leaders, purchased in June 2006 from the King estate. The papers and documents, written and collected by King from 1946 until his death in 1968, include copies of his "I Have a Dream" speech, his "Letter from a Birmingham Jail," his 1964 Nobel Peace Prize acceptance speech, and almost one hundred handwritten sermons.

The center, as envisioned, will be more than a museum of past events and accomplishments; it will be a living facility featuring speakers, art exhibits, conferences, films, theater performances, and educational programs.

In June 2007, the investment bank Goldman Sachs donated $2 million to Morehouse College to endow the Goldman Sachs Leadership Chair in Civil and Human Rights. Undoubtedly, there will be close cooperation between Morehouse and the Center for Civil and Human Rights in developing their respective programs. Also in June 2007, the proposed center received support in the form of a gift of $1 million from the Turner Broadcasting System.

The planners of the CCHR hope to break ground for the new facility in 2009 and to open it to the public in 2010. After it is open, a visit to the center would be an ideal way to begin or end the tours described in this guide.

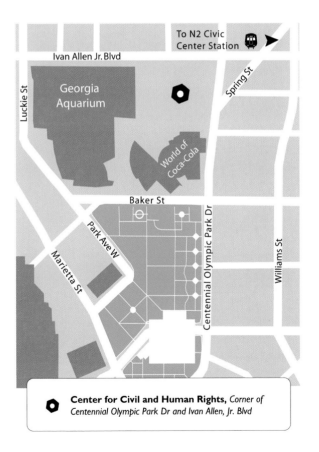

Center for Civil and Human Rights, *Corner of Centennial Olympic Park Dr and Ivan Allen, Jr. Blvd*

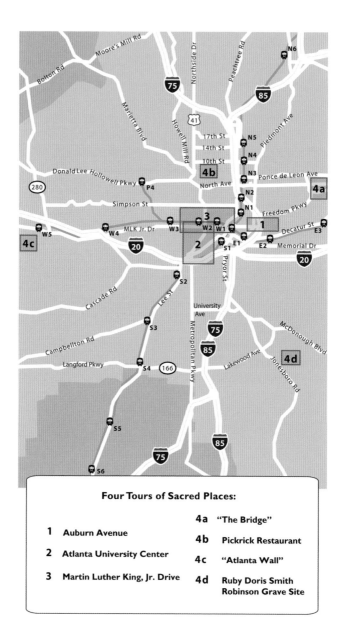

Four Tours of Sacred Places:

1   Auburn Avenue

2   Atlanta University Center

3   Martin Luther King, Jr. Drive

4a   "The Bridge"

4b   Pickrick Restaurant

4c   "Atlanta Wall"

4d   Ruby Doris Smith
      Robinson Grave Site

Four Tours
of the Civil Rights
Sites in Atlanta

There are four walking and driving tours detailed in the following pages. The first three explore sites located within a single neighborhood or along a specific street. Thus, visits to these sites could be organized as walking tours. Allow an hour and a half to two hours to complete each walking tour.

Each of the four sites discussed in Tour 4 is in a different quadrant of the city. These sites can be visited most conveniently by car although all four can be reached by public transportation.

Directions to the sites by car and public transportation are provided at the beginning of Tours 1–3 and, in Tour 4, at the beginning of the description of each site.

Auburn Avenue

DIRECTIONS BY CAR Take I-75/85 north or south to Freedom Parkway (Exit 248C). Go one block to Boulevard. At Boulevard turn right and follow the sign to the Martin Luther King, Jr., National Historic Site parking lot.

DIRECTIONS BY MARTA Take the #3 bus at the MARTA Five Points Station (M) to the Martin Luther King, Jr., Historic Site at 450 Auburn Avenue or take the east line train to the King Memorial Station (E2) and walk three blocks north to Auburn Avenue.[31]

After the Civil War, ex-slaves bought property east of the city's central business district in the low-lying area of what is now Auburn Avenue and Jesse Hill, Jr. Dr. (formerly Butler St.). Whites soon began to refer to the new black settlement as Darktown. At the time, Auburn was named Wheat Street, after white merchant Augustus Wheat. In 1893 the new residents successfully petitioned the city council to change the name to Auburn Avenue.

Before 1906 Auburn Avenue was a mixture of black and white residents and businesses, with whites still in the majority. However, after the 1906 Atlanta

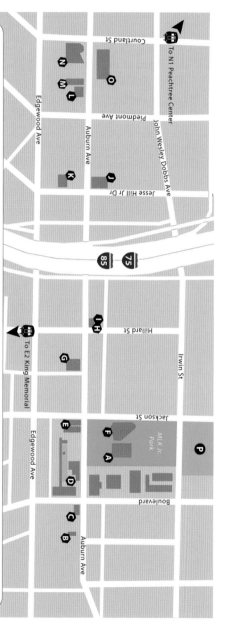

A Martin Luther King, Jr. National Historic Site, 450 Auburn Ave.

B Martin Luther King, Jr. Birth Home, 501 Auburn Ave.

C Fire Station # 6, 39 Boulevard

D Martin Luther King, Jr. Center, 449 Auburn Ave.

E Historic Ebenezer Baptist Church, 407 Auburn Ave.

F Ebenezer Baptist Church, 400 Auburn Ave.

G Wheat Street Baptist Church, 359 Auburn Ave.

H SCLC Office, 334 Auburn Ave.

I SCLC/W.O.M.E.N., Inc., 328 Auburn Ave.

J Big Bethel AME Church, 220 Auburn Ave.

K Butler Street YMCA, 20-24 Jesse Hill Jr. Dr.

L Atlanta Daily World, 145 Auburn Ave.

M APEX Museum, 135 Auburn Ave.

N Auburn Avenue Research Library, 101 Auburn Ave.

O Atlanta Life Insurance Company, 100 Auburn Ave.

P Visitor Parking

race riot, the city zoned the area a black area and Auburn Avenue soon became predominately black.[32]

During the 1920s and 1930s Auburn Avenue developed as the main street of black Atlanta. Although blacks lived, worked, and relaxed there as early as the late 1800s, by the 1920s and 1930s Auburn Avenue and surrounding streets had become the center of Atlanta's black business, entertainment, and social life. In the 1930s John Wesley Dobbs, a resident of nearby Houston Street and noted leader of the Prince Hall Masonic Order in Georgia, christened the neighborhood "Sweet Auburn." "There's nothing sweeter than money," he proclaimed, referring to the many prosperous businesses on Auburn Avenue. In 1934, following his retirement as a US Railroad Postal Clerk, Dobbs opened the Masonic Headquarters Office at 334 Auburn Avenue.[33]

Martin Luther King, Jr., National Historic Site

450 Auburn Ave., NE

www.nps.gov/malu

The Martin Luther King., Jr., National Historic Site, located directly across the street from the King Center, was opened in 1996.

Built and operated by the National Park Service, the Martin Luther King, Jr., National Historic Site provides information about Auburn Avenue, arranges tours of the King birth home, and maintains a civil rights museum. The centerpiece of the museum is laid out in the form of six circular modules, each

Martin Luther King, Jr., National Historic Site

describing with sound, pictures, and commentary the life and death of Martin Luther King, Jr., and the development of the civil rights movement. The six modules, titled "Courage to Lead: The Life of Martin Luther King, Jr.," are identified as: 1) Segregation; 2) King Family; 3) Call to Lead; 4) Visiting the Mountain; 5) Expanding the Dream; and 6) Overcoming Loss. In the center of the six modules is a life-size diorama of figures on a freedom march. Visitors are permitted to join the figures as they "march."

Also in the museum is the mule-drawn farm wagon used to carry King's casket the 4.3 miles from Ebenezer Church to Morehouse College on the afternoon of his funeral on April 9, 1968. Two hundred thousand mourners followed the caisson in a funeral cortege that lasted nearly three hours. Another 120 million watched the proceedings on television. When the marchers reached Morehouse, 50,000 mourners crowded onto the quadrangle shared by Morehouse and Atlanta University. **(SEE TOUR 2 FOR MORE DETAILS ON THE MEMORIAL SERVICE.)**

The Historic Site has an auditorium, which is used for films and lectures, and a gallery where exhibits related to the civil rights movement and human rights are mounted. There is also a gift shop that sells books, tapes, and posters. The museum and most exhibits are free to the public.

Behind the museum building is a larger-than-life-size statue of Mahatma Gandhi shown in a walking stride and carrying a walking stick. The statue was sculpted by Ram Sutar of New Delhi, India, and was donated to the site by the Indian Council for Cultural Relations in India, the National Federation of Indian-American Associations, and the Indian Embassy in the United States. Civil rights leader Andrew Young dedicated the statue on January 24, 1998.

King was greatly influenced by Gandhi. For example, in his book about the Montgomery Bus Boycott, King said, "Christ furnished the spirit and motivation, while Gandhi furnished the method."[34]

Also behind the museum building is the International Civil Rights Walk of Fame, which contains black marble sidewalk plaques engraved with the shoe-prints of selected "soldiers of justice." Sponsored by the Trumpet Awards Foundation, the shoe-prints are made from shoes donated by the honorees. Begun in 2003 by Xernona Clayton, founder and executive producer of the Trumpet Awards, the Walk of Fame contained sixty-two shoe-prints as of 2008. Following are the identities of the sixty-two honorees with the year of their induction:

Gandhi Statue

2004

Juanita J. Abernathy and **Rev. Ralph David Abernathy, Sr.** (1926–1990), co-workers with Martin Luther King, Jr.; Atlanta mayor **Ivan Allen, Jr.** (1911–2003); **Julian Bond**, SNCC activist and NAACP board president; **President Jimmy Carter**; **Medgar Evers** (1925–1963), who was murdered in Mississippi in 1963; **Dorothy Height,** president of the National Council of Negro Women; **Jesse L. Jackson, Sr.**, founder and president of the Rainbow PUSH Coalition; **Judge Frank M. Johnson** (1918–1999); **President Lyndon B. Johnson** (1908–1973); SNCC activist and US Representative **John**

Lewis; **Evelyn G. Lowery**, founder and chair of SCLC/W.O.M.E.N; **Joseph E. Lowery**, president of SCLC; Supreme Court **Justice Thurgood Marshall** (1908–1993); civil rights icon **Rosa Parks** (1913–2005); civil rights leader **Hosea Williams** (1926–2000); **Andrew Young**, US congressman, UN ambassador and Atlanta mayor.

2005

baseball great **Henry ("Hank") Aaron**; singer **Harry Belafonte**; US representative **John Conyers, Jr.**; comedian **Dick Gregory**; Atlanta mayor **Maynard H. Jackson, Jr.** (1938–2003); **Ralph E. McGill** (1898–1969), editor of the *Atlanta Journal Constitution*; **Rev. Fred L. Shuttlesworth**, founder and leader of the Alabama Christian Movement for Human Rights; Atlanta Braves owner and media mogul **Ted Turner**; **Judge Elbert P. Tuttle, Sr.** (1897–1996); singer **Nancy Wilson**; labor and church leader **Rev. Addie L. Wyatt**.

2006

Rev. Joseph E. Boone (1922–2006), co–worker with Martin Luther King, Jr. in SCLC; **Rev. William Holmes Borders** (1905–1993), pastor, Wheat Street Baptist Church; **Xenona Clayton**, co–worker with Martin Luther King, Jr.; **President William J. Clinton**; singer and entertainer

Lena Horne; **John E. Jacob,** executive vice president of Anheuser–Busch Company; SCLC organizer **Rev. James Orange** (1942–2008); **Bernard C. Parks,** member of Los Angeles City Council; South African **Arch Bishop Desmond Tutu**; singer **Stevie Wonder**.

2007

author and journalist **Lerone Bennett Jr.**; singer and entertainer **Tony Bennett**; **Marian Wright Edelman,** founder and president of the Children's Defense Fund; Atlanta mayor **Shirley Franklin**; lawyer **Frankie Muse Freeman**, who championed school and housing desegregation in St. Louis; boxing great **Joe Louis** (1914–1981); **Rev. Otis Moss, Jr.**, civil rights activist and pastor of Mt. Olivet Institutional Baptist Church in Cleveland, Ohio; Bahamian Prime Minister **Sir Lynden Pindling** (1930–2000); actor **Sidney Poitier**; **Otis Smith** (1925–2007), first black practicing pediatrician in Georgia; US Representative **Maxine Waters**; **L. Douglas Wilder,** the first black governor of Virginia; **Jean Childs Young** (1933–1994), educator and human rights activist.

2008

Maya Angelou, poet, actress, and author; US Senator **Edward W. Brooke**; **Tyrone L. Brooks, Sr.**, civil rights worker and Georgia representative; singer, dancer, and actor **Sammy Davis, Jr.** (1925–1990); **Jesse Hill, Jr.**, business executive and first black president of the Atlanta Chamber of Commerce; **Benjamin Hooks**, executive director of the NAACP, 1977–1992; **Clarence B. Jones**, attorney, speech writer, fund raiser, and confidant of Martin Luther King, Jr.; **Tom Joyner**, host of *The Tom Joyner Morning Show*; the **Right Honorable Michael Manley** (1924–1997), prime minister of Jamaica; **Herman Russell, Sr.**, founder and CEO of H. J. Russell & Company; **Wyatt Tee Walker**, executive director of the SCLC, 1960–1964, and pastor of Canaan Baptist Church in Harlem.

DR. MAYA ANGELOU

Martin Luther King, Jr. Birth Home

Martin Luther King, Jr., Birth Home

501 Auburn Ave. NE

www.nps.gov/features/malu/feat0001/BirthHomeTour

This two-story Queen Anne Style house was built in
1895. In 1909, the Reverend A. D. Williams, pastor
of Ebenezer Baptist Church, bought the house for
$3500 and moved into the house with his wife,
Jennie, and daughter, Alberta. In 1926, Alberta
married the Reverend Martin Luther King (Sr.) and
moved into the upstairs. They had three children
while living there: Christine, Martin Luther, Jr.
(born January 15, 1929), and Alfred Daniel. The
birth home is open for tours daily led by park
rangers from the National Park Service. Visitors must
register for a tour of the birth home at the visitors'
desk at the NPS historic site at 450 Auburn Avenue.

After the death of Mrs. Williams in 1941, the family moved a few blocks north to 193 Boulevard. The house at 193 Boulevard was demolished in the 1960s for the construction of the Stone Mountain Expressway, now known as Freedom Parkway.

Fire Station No. 6 Museum

Fire Station No. 6 Museum

39 Boulevard, NE

This Romanesque Revival Style station, constructed in 1894, was one of the original eight fire stations in Atlanta and is Atlanta's oldest standing firehouse. It played an important role in extinguishing the Great Atlanta Fire of 1917, which destroyed much of the central section of Auburn Avenue. Young Martin Luther King, Jr., spent many hours here playing and talking to the firemen. No longer an active fire station, it recently has been restored by the National Park Service and the City of Atlanta and is operated by the Park Service as a bookstore and information center. The bookstore carries many books and materials relevant to King and the civil rights movement.

The Martin Luther King, Jr., Center for Nonviolent Social Change, Inc.

449 Auburn Ave., NE

www.thekingcenter.org

Coretta Scott King, widow of Martin Luther King, Jr., founded the King Center in 1968. Following his funeral on April 9, 1968, King was buried in a crypt in South-View Cemetery on the south side of Atlanta. In the early 1970s, the crypt was moved from South-View to its current site at the King Center. The new site, with a reflecting pool and nearby eternal flame, was dedicated in 1977.

Crypt of Dr. Martin Luther King, Jr., and Coretta Scott King

Mrs. King died on January 30, 2006, at the age of seventy-eight. Five days later, on February 4, mourners silently passed by her casket as she lay in state in the Georgia State Capitol rotunda (the first woman and the first African American in Georgia so honored). Following her funeral a the New Birth Missionary Baptist Church in DeKalb County, her remains were placed in a temporary crypt in a flower garden near the eternal flame at the King Center. Ten months later, on November 20, she was moved to lie beside her husband in a new, enlarged double crypt on an island in the center of the reflecting pool. The two epitaphs on the new crypt read as follows, "REV. MARTIN LUTHER KING, Jr., 1929–1968. 'Free at last, Free at last, Thank God Almighty I'm Free at last'" and "CORETTA SCOTT KING 1927–2006. 'And now abide Faith, Hope, Love, these three; but the greatest of these is Love.' I Cor. 13:13.'"

In addition to the crypt, the King Center has a small museum, rooms dedicated to Rosa Parks and Gandhi, a gift shop, an auditorium, and offices. A library and archives contain materials relevant to the civil rights movement, including many of King's papers and the papers of the Southern Christian Leadership Conference (SCLC), the Student Nonviolent Coordinating Committee (SNCC), and the Congress of Racial Equality (CORE). Also, the library has a variety of audio-visual and oral history collections. Materials are available for library use only.

Historic Ebenezer Baptist Church
(Heritage Sanctuary)

407 Auburn Ave., NE

www.historicebenezer.org

The Reverend John A. Parker founded Ebenezer as a congregation on nearby Airline Street in 1886. The present Gothic Revival structure was built 1914–22.

For more than eighty years, the ministers of Ebenezer were members of three generations of the same family: A. D. Williams (Martin Luther King, Sr.'s father-in-law), Martin Luther King, Sr., and Martin Luther King, Jr. King, Sr., served as pastor from 1931–1975. King, Jr., joined his father ("Daddy King") as co-pastor in 1960 and served with him until his death in 1968. (King, Jr., had been ordained in the church in 1948, when he was a senior at Morehouse College.)

In 1957, while still pastor of Dexter Avenue Baptist Church in Montgomery, Alabama, Dr. King convened sixty black ministers from ten states at Ebenezer to discuss plans for the integration of public transportation. At a follow-up meeting in

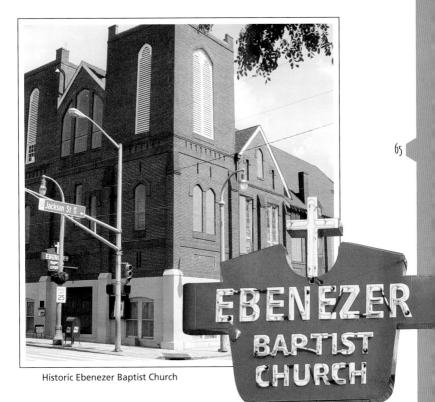

Historic Ebenezer Baptist Church

New Orleans a month later, the group founded the Southern Christian Leadership Conference (SCLC). During the eight years of his tenure at Ebenezer, Dr. King preached many sermons about social justice and human rights and used the church for many meetings related to the civil rights movement.

Martin Luther King, Jr.'s funeral was held at Ebenezer on April 9, 1968. Only 750 mourners were able to crowd into the sanctuary. Two hundred thousand others gathered outside the church and listened on loud speakers as inside they played excerpts from a tape of the sermon, "The Drum Major Instinct" that King had preached at Ebenezer on February 4, just two months earlier.

SACRED PLACES   AUBURN AVENUE

The Drum Major Instinct

I'd like somebody to mention that day that Martin Luther King, Jr., tried to give his life serving others.

I'd like for somebody to say that day that Martin Luther King, Jr., tried to love somebody.

I want you to say that day that I tried to be right on the war question.

I want you to be able to say that day that I did try to feed the hungry.

And I want you to be able to say that day that I did try in my life to clothe those who were naked.

I want you to say on that day that I did try in my life to visit those who were in prison.

I want you to say that I tried to love and serve humanity.

Yes, if you want to say that I was a drum major, say that I was a drum major for justice. Say that I was a drum major for peace. I was a drum major for righteousness. And all of the other shallow things will not matter.[35]

Initially, King was buried in an aboveground marble crypt in South-View Cemetery. In the early 1970s the crypt was relocated to an island in the reflecting pool at the King Center right next to the church. After his wife, Coretta, died in January 2006, a new double crypt was constructed, and Coretta joined her husband on November 20, 2006.

After the new Ebenezer Church was built in 1999, historic Ebenezer became a tourist site operated by the National Park Service. However, the Heritage Sanctuary is still occasionally used for services and meetings. The church is open to the public free of charge. (In 2008 the sanctuary was closed in order to restore it as it was in the 1960s. It will reopen Spring, 2009.)

New Ebenezer Baptist Church

New Ebenezer Baptist Church
(Horizon Sanctuary)

400 Auburn Ave., NE

www.historicebenezer.org/home.html

At 9:00 A.M. on Sunday, March 7, 1999, the Ebenezer congregation exited the old 600-seat Heritage Sanctuary and walked across Auburn Avenue for their first service in the new 1,800-seat Horizon Sanctuary.

Unlike the rectangular shape of the old sanctuary, the new sanctuary is fan-shaped—broadest at the rear and narrowing to focus on a stage for the pastor and choir. Behind the choir, at the highest point and covered by a dome, is the baptismal pool. A ceiling skylight runs along the peak of the roof, and tall, arched windows adorn the sides. Ten of the sanctuary columns have box-like structures at their bases, each adorned with a symbol of the Coptic "Ebenezer Cross" used in Ethiopia. The upholstery and carpets are designed to resemble African textiles. Future plans for the sanctuary include replacing the current clear-glass windows with stained-glass windows depicting stories of West Africa, the Middle Passage, Slavery, and the Great Migration from the South to the North.

In front of the entrance to the church stands a bell tower that is fifty-five feet tall. The church is situated so that the axis of the church is in direct line with the King crypts just across the street.

The Reverend Joseph L. Roberts succeeded Martin Luther King, Sr., as pastor in 1975 ("Daddy King" died in 1984) and served until September 2005. On October 1, 2005, the Reverend Raphael Gamaliel Warnock was installed as Ebenezer's fifth senior pastor. The church is not open to the public except for scheduled services.

As you leave the New Ebenezer Baptist Church, note the statue close to the sidewalk in front of the church. Named "Behold," the ten-foot bronze monument represents the ancient African ritual of holding a newborn child up to the heavens and declaring, "Behold the only thing bigger than yourself." Specifically, the statue represents the baptism of Kissy by her father, Kunte Kinte, the character made famous in Alex Haley's book Roots. On the granite base of the monument, sculptor Patrick Morelli inscribed the words, "Dedicated to the Memory of Dr. Martin Luther King, Jr., for His Moral Courage and Nobility of Spirit." Coretta Scott King unveiled the monument at its current location on January 11, 1990, as a tribute to her late husband and as an inspiration to all who fight for dignity, social justice, and human rights.

"Behold" Statue

Wheat Street Baptist Church

Wheat Street Baptist Church

359 Auburn Ave., NE

www.wheatstreetbaptist.org

Robert E. Pharrow, a local black contractor, began building this Gothic Revival building in 1920. It was completed in 1939.

From 1937, until his retirement in 1988, Williams Holmes Borders preached from the church's pulpit and served the congregation as pastor. In the 1940s, teenaged Martin Luther King, Jr., would sometimes sneak away from his home church, Ebenezer Baptist, walk the few blocks to Wheat Street Baptist and sit in the balcony to listen to Rev. Borders preach.

In 1943 Borders wrote a poem to affirm and cele-brate the many contributions of African Americans. He titled it, "I Am Somebody." Later, during the civil rights movement and beyond, Jesse Jackson used the phrase as a popular rallying cry in his sermons and speeches.

Early in his tenure as pastor at Wheat Street Baptist, Borders provided leadership for African Americans struggling for civil rights. In 1946, he presided at the funeral for several black servicemen who had been lynched at the Moore's Ford Bridge in Monroe, Georgia (sixty miles east of Atlanta), and raised money to track down their killers. In January 1957, as part of the Triple L Movement (Love, Law, and Liberation) that he had helped organize, he and a group of black ministers were arrested for sitting in the "white" sections of the city's trolleys and buses.

During the 1960s, Borders enthusiastically supported the Atlanta University Center students as they sat-in, kneeled-in, marched, and picketed. He opened his church to them for meetings and rallies. For example, in May 1960, he welcomed the students when they were turned away from the state capitol. He also organized many meetings at his church in support of Martin Luther King, Jr.

Southern Christian Leadership Conference (SCLC) National Office

334 Auburn Ave., NE

www.sclcnational.org

The Prince Hall Masons of Georgia built this building in 1940. Under the leadership of John Wesley Dobbs, the building served as the Masons' headquarters for many years. In 1965, the eastern

New SCLC Headquarters

part of the building became the headquarters of the Southern Christian Leadership Conference, the organization that Martin Luther King, Jr., helped found in 1957 and led as president from 1957 until his death in 1968. The SCLC office initially was in the Savoy Hotel (formerly at 239 Auburn). Later, it moved to 208 Auburn, then to 41 Exchange Place downtown, before locating to this building in 1965. In 2001, SCLC moved its office to 591-A Edgewood Avenue and, then, in 2006, to a temporary office at 600 West Peachtree Street. In 2007, a $3 million international headquarters was built immediately west of the old SCLC office at 320 Auburn Avenue. The new 12,500-square-foot, two-story building will house SCLC offices as well as shops and restaurants.

After King's death in 1968, Ralph David Abernathy was elected president of SCLC and served until 1977. Subsequent presidents were Joseph E. Lowery, 1977–1997; Martin L. King, III, 1997–2004; Fred Shuttlesworth, February 2004–November 2004; and Charles Steele, Jr., November 2004–present.

SCLC Office, 1965–2001

In March 2008, Emory University purchased a portion of the SCLC archives. After the thousands of photographs, letters, business records, speeches, and field reports are processed, they will be available to the public in the Special Collections section of the Robert W. Woodruff Library at Emory University (http://marbl.library.emory.edu).

SCLC/W.O.M.E.N., Inc.
(Women's Organizational Movement for Equality Now)

328 Auburn Ave., NE

www.sclcwomeninc.org

SCLC/W.O.M.E.N., Inc., was founded in 1979 by Evelyn Gibson Lowery. The purpose of the organization is "to champion the rights of women, children, families, and responding to the problems of the disenfranchised regardless of ethnicity, gender, age, or religion."[36] Major programs include education, employment skills training, literacy training, and health education with a specific emphasis on HIV/AIDS infection and child abuse and neglect awareness.

The organization actively promotes education about the civil rights movement. Twice a year SCLC/W.O.M.E.N., Inc. organizes a tour to the 1950s, 1960s, and 1970s civil rights sites in Alabama, including Birmingham, Marion, Selma, Whitehall, Montgomery, and Tuskegee. Also, Mrs. Lowery and SCLC/W.O.M.E.N., Inc. have constructed twelve memorials to honor those "who sacrificed and gave their lives to the movement."[37]

SCLC/W.O.M.E.N. Memorials in Alabama

Viola Gregg Liuzzo, along U.S. Highway 80 at the spot where she was killed in 1965 (1991); **Jimmie Lee Jackson**, Marion (1991); **Earl T. Shinhoster**, along Highway 85 close to Tuskegee (2001); **Albert Turner, Sr.**, Marion (2001); **The Civil Rights Freedom Wall of Perry County**, Marion (2002); **Rev. James Orange**, Marion (2002); **Rev. Hosea Williams** (2002) and **John Lewis** (2004), both at the foot of the Edmund Pettus Bridge in Selma; **The Civil Rights Freedom Wall of the City of Selma, Dallas County, Alabama**, in front of Brown Chapel AME Church in Selma (2005); **Marie Foster/Amelia Boynton Robinson**, at the foot of the Edmund Pettus Bridge in Selma (2005); **Rev. James Reeb**, on Washington Street in Selma (2005); and **Rosa Parks**, at the entrance to Montgomery State University in Montgomery, Alabama (2006).

Viola Liuzzo Memorial

SCLC/W.O.M.E.N., Inc. Office Buildng

The building in which the SCLC/W.O.M.E.N's office is located was built in 1927 by the Grand Temple and Tabernacle International Order of Twelve Knights and Daughters of Tabor, Jurisdiction of Georgia. For a number of years, the building housed radio station WERD, the first black-owned radio station in the United States, which began broadcasting in 1949.

Big Bethel AME Church

220 Auburn Ave., NE

www.bigbethelame.org

Big Bethel grew out of the Bethel Tabernacle, a church organized for slaves by Methodist slave-holders before the Civil War. In 1865 the Tabernacle became affiliated with the African Methodist Episcopal (AME) Church. The present structure was begun in 1891 and completed in 1921. Although it escaped the ravages of the Great Atlanta Fire of 1917, it was gutted by fire in 1922, the day after the church's insurance expired. Because of its granite construction the walls survived. With help from the city, the interior was quickly rebuilt.

On January 1, 1957, less than a month after the conclusion of the successful bus boycott led by Martin Luther King, Jr., in Montgomery, Alabama, the Atlanta chapter of the NAACP organized an afternoon rally at Big Bethel to discuss the ending of segregation practices in Atlanta. The group packed the sanctuary and spilled into the corridors, the basement, and the sidewalks outside the church. After the reading of the Fourteenth Amendment and

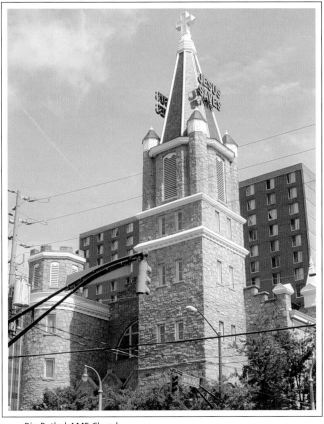

Big Bethel AME Church

excerpts from the Emancipation Proclamation,
Dr. King, who had come from Montgomery for the
meeting, spoke. During his speech, King made reference to the Montgomery bus boycott and how the
Negro citizens there walked "in pride rather than
ride in humiliation" and stressed that the same could
happen in Atlanta. He said it was important that the
Negro race stick together and stand up for their rights
as given them by the Constitution of the United
States. Following King's speech, Martin Luther King,
Sr., made an appeal for donations. About $7,000
was raised.

Big Bethel is renowned for its annual production of "We're Heaven Bound," a drama in song and verse that recounts the experiences of twenty-four pilgrims as they resist Satan's temptations on their way to the Promised Land. The drama, reminiscent of John Bunyan's Pilgrim's Progress, is directed, acted, and sung by the combined choirs of Big Bethel. Originally written by Lula Jones and Nellie Davis, the play was first performed in 1930 and is undoubtedly the longest-running black drama ever produced.[38]

In 1881, Morris Brown College (named after AME bishop Morris Brown) was founded in the basement of Big Bethel. The college formally opened four years later when 107 students and nine teachers moved into a crude wooden structure at the corner of Boulevard and Houston Streets. Later, a multistory brick building replaced the wooden structure. The college remained at the corner of Boulevard and Houston until 1933 when it moved to its present location at 643 Martin Luther King, Jr. Drive, SW.

Butler Street YMCA

20–24 Jesse Hill, Jr. Dr., NE (formerly Butler St.)

www.butlerstreetymca.org

The Butler Street YMCA is one of the oldest YMCA organizations in the country owned and operated by African-Americans. The founding meeting of the organization was held in the basement of Wheat Street Baptist. The Reverend J. S. Brandon, a member of the church, convened the meeting. Brandon subsequently was elected the first president

Butler Street YMCA

of the new organization. For the next several decades, the organization occupied several locations on Auburn Avenue before moving to its current location on Jesse Hill, Jr. Drive.

The building at 20–24 Jesse Hill, Jr. Dr. was completed in 1922 and soon offered an array of services for men and boys, including counseling; debates; lectures; club, reading, and dormitory rooms; showers; telephones; and a gymnasium.

Beginning in the 1940s, and continuing for decades, the Butler Street YMCA played a vital role in the development of civil rights in Atlanta. In 1944, after the US Supreme Court's decision outlawing whites-only voting in political primaries, Mayor Hartsfield met with black leaders at the YMCA and worked out plans to register blacks. In 1945, the YMCA established the Hungry Club Forum, which was designed to be "Food for Taste and Food for Thought for Those Who Hunger for

Information and Association." The Hungry Club was one of the few places in Atlanta where blacks and whites could meet together to discuss plans for desegregation. The forum still meets weekly and continues to provide a venue for a discussion of public and civic affairs. In 1948, when the Atlanta Police Department hired its first eight black policemen but denied them access to the facilities at the main police station, the YMCA offered them its own facilities and permitted them to shower and change clothes there.

Many Atlanta civil rights leaders, including Martin Luther King, Jr., Julian Bond, Andrew Young, and John Lewis, were nurtured at the Butler Street "Y" and used it to gain political and social experience. King often used the pool to relax and unwind from his strenuous schedule. Jesse Hill, Jr., the longtime president of the Atlanta Life Insurance Company and the man after whom the street was renamed, called the Butler Street YMCA the "Black City Hall of Atlanta."

In 1994, a new $1.6 million, 13,000-square-foot building was opened on the east side of Jesse Hill, Jr., Dr. The old building, however, continues to operate as a part of the organization.

The small building attached to the north side of the old building is the A. T. Walden building. Walden, one of the few African Americans practicing law in Georgia in the 1960s, served as one of the two major lawyers for the students arrested in the movement (the other was Donald Hollowell). Walden also chaired the executive boards of the Butler Street YMCA and the Atlanta Urban League and served as president of the Atlanta branch of the National Association for the Advancement of Colored People (NAACP).

Atlanta Daily World

145 Auburn Ave., NE

The Atlanta Daily World is the oldest black-owned daily newspaper in the United States. Founded in 1928 by William A. Scott, the newspaper has been owned and managed by the Scott family for eight decades. Among those who worked at the Daily World were Bob Johnson, editor of Jet magazine; Lerone Bennett, Jr., editor of Ebony magazine and the author of many books on black history and civil rights, including Before the Mayflower: A History of the Negro in America, 1619–1964 and What Manner of Man: A Biography of Martin Luther King, Jr; and Harry McAlphin, the first black journalist on the White House press corps.

Atlanta Daily World Office

When the sit-ins and civil rights demonstrations began in the 1960s, the Scotts, who were conservative Republicans, often refused to publish information about the students' activities, or, if they did publish news items, they editorialized against what the students were doing. So the students decided to start their own newspaper. They named it the Atlanta Inquirer and published their first issue on July 31, 1960. Both newspapers are still in publication today as weeklies.

In March 2008, a tornado roared through downtown Atlanta, leaving a path of destruction in its wake. Among the many buildings hit was the Atlanta Daily World building. The winds tore off the marquee in the front of the building and damaged the offices inside. Because of the damage, the staff was forced to relocate temporarily. As of August 2008, it is not known when the office will again be open for business.

APEX
African-American Panoramic Experience Museum

135 Auburn Ave., NE

www.apexmuseum.org

The African-American Panoramic Experience (APEX) was founded in 1978 by Dan Moore. The museum's mission is to "present history from an African-American perspective"[39] and to help visitors appreciate the contributions of African Americans to the United States and the world. It advertises itself as the place "Where Every Month is Black History

APEX Museum

Month."[40] The museum contains a gallery, a video theater, and exhibition space. Two recent exhibits were "The Georgia Negro: A Social Study," which displayed photographs and commentary from W. E. B. Du Bois's exhibit at the 1900 Paris Exhibition, and "Still I Rise," which featured artifacts of slavery and "the resistance of a people that triumphed through insurmountable odds."[41]

A permanent exhibit in the museum is a replica of the Yates & Milton Drug Store, which was opened in 1923 in the Odd Fellows Building at the corner of Auburn and Butler Street (now Jesse Hill, Jr. Dr.). Established by black businessmen Clayton R. Yates and Lorimer D. Milton, the drug store was a popular place to shop or to take one's date for a drink at the soda fountain.

The museum charges a small admission fee and is closed on Mondays.

Auburn Avenue Research Library

Auburn Avenue Research Library

101 Auburn Ave., NE

www.af.public.lib.ga.us/aarl

The Auburn Avenue Research Library (AARL) is a special branch of the Atlanta-Fulton Public Library System. Opened in 1994, the library offers "reference and archival collections for the study and research of African cultures."[42] The library also organizes and hosts a variety of events and services such as seminars, lectures, workshops, discussions, and book signings. On the main floor of the library is the Cary-McPheeters Gallery, where exhibits of national and international importance are mounted.

The library has many materials related to the civil rights movement, including microfilm copies of the Student Nonviolent Coordinating Committee (SNCC) archives and the papers (documents, photos, letters, etc.) of civil rights leader Andrew Young, Jr.

The library is free and open to the public. However, the library's holdings can be used only in the library; there are no checkout privileges.

Atlanta Life Insurance Company

100 Auburn Ave., NE

www.atlantalife.com

The Atlanta Life Insurance Company was founded in 1905 by Alonzo F. Herndon. Born a slave in Social Circle, Georgia, in 1858, Herndon arrived in Atlanta in 1882 (at the age of twenty-four) and opened three barbershops for whites, the most notable of which was the Tonsorial Palace on Peachtree Street. With his wealth from the barber-shops and real estate investments, Herndon became Atlanta's first black millionaire. In 1905 he purchased the Atlanta Protective and Benevolent Association for $140, which he reorganized into the Atlanta Life Insurance Company. The new company soon developed into Atlanta's largest black business, and today (known as Atlanta Life) is the largest black-owned insurance company in the United States. Although Herndon was not openly active in racial or civil rights issues, he shared much of his wealth with the black community.

In 1893, Herndon married Adrienne McNeil. Together, the young couple designed a Beaux Arts Classical mansion for themselves. Unfortunately, Adrienne died in 1910, just a week before the house was completed. The house still stands at 587 University Place, NW, near Morris Brown College.
(SEE TOUR 3 FOR A PHOTOGRAPH AND DETAILS OF THE HERNDON HOME.)

Old Atlanta Life Insurance Office

New Atlanta Life Insurance Office

Herndon married Jessie Gillespie in 1912, and the new couple and Alonzo and Adrienne's son, Norris, moved into the new house. Later Norris succeeded his father as president of Atlanta Life.

In 1918, the Atlanta Life Insurance Company built an office building at 148 Auburn Avenue. That building is still standing but is no longer in use. In 1980 the company built a larger and modern headquarters, known as Herndon Plaza, right next door, at 100 Auburn Avenue.

As early as the 1940s and 1950s, the officials of Atlanta Life used their influence to support the civil rights efforts in Atlanta. When the Atlanta University students initiated sit-ins and boycotts in 1960, the Atlanta Life officials supported their efforts. In particular, Jesse Hill, Jr., who became president of Atlanta Life in 1973, supported and advised the students. In July 1960, he helped them launch the Atlanta Inquirer. Also, Hill and other Atlanta Life officials quietly provided bail money for many of the students who were arrested.

2

Atlanta University Center District

DIRECTIONS BY CAR FROM THE EAST Take I-20 west to the Lee Street exit (Exit 55B). Turn right onto Lee Street and continue through the next traffic light (Lee Street becomes Westview Drive). Park in the Spelman College parking deck on your immediate right.

DIRECTIONS BY CAR FROM THE WEST Take I-20 east to the Joseph Lowery Blvd. exit (Exit 55A). Cross Lowery and continue to the next traffic light. Turn left at Lee Street and continue through the next two traffic lights. Park in the Spelman College parking deck on your immediate right.

DIRECTIONS BY MARTA Take the south line train to the West End Station (S2). Exit the station and walk north on Lee Street to the Atlanta University Center. During the school year, shuttle buses run from the station to the schools in the AUC.

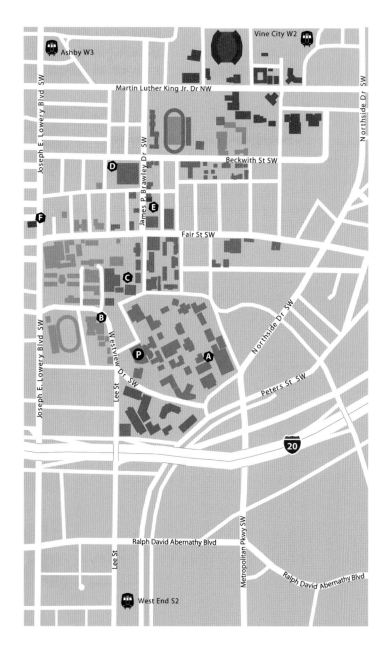

Ashby W3

Vine City W2

Martin Luther King Jr. Dr NW

Joseph E. Lowery Blvd SW

Northside Dr SW

Beckwith St SW

D

James P. Brawley Dr SW

E

F

Fair St SW

C

Northside Dr SW

B

Peters St SW

P

A

Westview Dr SW

Lee St

Joseph E. Lowery Blvd SW

20

Ralph David Abernathy Blvd

Lee St

Metropolitan Pkwy SW

Ralph David Abernathy Blvd

West End S2

Sites on Tour:

🅐 **Sisters Chapel (Spelman College),** *350 Spelman Ln.*

🅑 **The Martin Luther King Jr. International Chapel Plaza (Morehouse College),** *830 Westview Dr.*
   - Martin Luther King Statue
   - "I Have A Dream" Plaque
   - Howard Thurman Obelisk and Burial Site

🅒 **Clark Atlanta University/Morehouse College Quadrangle,** *223 James P. Brawley Dr.*
   - 40th-Anniversary Plaque
   - Site of Martin Luther King, Jr. Memorial Service
   - Benjamin E. Mays Statue and Crypt

🅓 **Robert W. Woodruff Library (Atlanta University Center),** *111 James P. Brawley Dr.*

🅔 **Rush Memorial Congregational Church,** *150 James P. Brawley Dr.*

🅕 **Warren Memorial United Methodist Church,** *181 Joseph Lowery*

Atlanta University Center Campuses:

▨ **Morehouse School of Medicine,** *720 Westview Dr.*

▨ **Spelman College,** *350 Spelman Ln.*

▨ **Morehouse College,** *830 Westview Dr.*

▨ **Clark Atlanta University,** *223 James P. Brawley Dr.*

▨ **Interdenominational Theological Center,** *700 MLK, Jr. Dr.*

▨ **Morris Brown College,** *643 Martin Luther King, Jr. Dr.*

🅟 **Spelman Parking Deck**

Many of the civil rights actions in Atlanta in the late 1950s and 1960s were planned and carried out by students and faculty at the Atlanta University Center (AUC), a consortium of six institutions in southwest Atlanta: Atlanta University, Clark College, Morehouse College, Morris Brown College, Spelman College, and the Interdenominational Theological Center (ITC).

Each of the six institutions developed independently (and at locations other than their current ones). However, in 1929 Atlanta University, Morehouse, and Spelman signed an Agreement of Affiliation that set up a system of cooperation in which Morehouse and Spelman offered undergraduate degrees and Atlanta University offered graduate degrees. The three other institutions joined the consortium later—Morris Brown and Clark in 1957 and the Interdenominational Theological Center (an affiliation of several seminaries) in 1959.

Since the 1960s, the makeup of the consortium has changed. In 1988 Clark and Atlanta University merged and became Clark Atlanta University (CAU), and, in 2003, Morris Brown College (643 Martin Luther King, Jr. Dr., SW) lost its accreditation and is no longer a part of the consortium. Today the consortium comprises only four institutions—Clark Atlanta University (223 James P. Brawley Dr., SW), Interdenominational Theological Center (700 Martin Luther King, Jr. Dr., SW), Morehouse College (830 Westview Dr., SW), and Spelman College (350 Spelman Ln., SW). However, in 1983 the Morehouse School of Medicine opened at 720 Westview Dr., across the street from Spelman, and, although not technically a part of the Atlanta University Center, is closely associated with it.

The presidents of the six schools during the years of the civil rights movement were Rufus Clement, Atlanta University; James P. Brawley, Clark; Benjamin E. Mays, Morehouse; James Cunningham, Morris Brown; Albert E. Manley, Spelman; and Harry V. Richardson, Interdenominational Theological Center. Among the six presidents, President Mays was the most supportive of the students' and faculty members' civil rights actions.

The AUC students and faculty who participated in the civil rights movement in Atlanta in the 1960s organized and coordinated their actions through the Committee On Appeal For Human Rights (COAHR), an organization the students founded in March 1960. However, the students and faculty did not restrict their civil rights actions to Atlanta. They also participated in campaigns and actions outside of Atlanta, including Rock Hill, South Carolina; Birmingham, Selma, and Montgomery, Alabama; Jackson, Laurel, and McComb, Mississippi; Albany and Macon, Georgia; Jacksonville, Florida; and Washington, D.C., among others.

A number of buildings and locations on the AUC campuses have significant connections to the civil rights movement. The following pages identify those buildings and locations and discuss their relevance to the civil rights movement.

Sisters Chapel
(Spelman College)

350 Spelman Ln., SW

Activists planned and evaluated demonstrations—and prayed for jailed demonstrators—in Sisters Chapel. Also, Martin Luther King, Jr., lay in state in Sisters Chapel for the two days before his funeral on April 9, 1968. At the time, King's alma mater, Morehouse College, did not have a big enough chapel to accommodate the crowd of eighty thousand mourners who passed by his casket.

Built in 1927, Sisters Chapel honors the lives of Laura Spelman Rockefeller, wife of John D. Rockefeller, and her sister, Lucy Maria Spelman. The college is named after the Spelman family who, along with the Rockefellers, provided financial and moral support to the school in its fledgling years.

Winding line of mourners filing into Sisters Chapel to view the body of Martin Luther King, Jr., April 7, 1968.

SACRED PLACES   ATLANTA UNIVERSITY CENTER DISTRICT

Sisters Chapel, 2008

Martin Luther King., Jr.
International Chapel Plaza

(Morehouse College)

830 Westview Dr., SW

The Martin Luther King, Jr., International Chapel was built in 1978. On the plaza in front of the chapel are three artistic objects significant to the civil rights movement. The most obvious is the larger-than-life statue of Martin Luther King, Jr. The statue, sculpted by Edward J. Dwight, shows the standing King literally pointing to Morehouse College, his alma mater, and metaphorically pointing to the north, which, for African Americans, symbolized freedom during slavery and the Great Migration from the South to the North during the decades spanning the 1920s to the 1960s.

Attached to the north side of the chapel is a bronze plaque engraved with King's "I Have a Dream" speech, delivered at the march on Washington on August 28, 1963. On the lower level in back of the

King Chapel, Morehouse College

chapel is a small museum with numerous pictures and other materials highlighting King's actions in the civil rights movement. Dr. Lawrence E. Carter, Sr., is dean of the chapel and responsible for the museum's creation and maintenance.

Look to the right of the King statue, to the far west side of the Chapel plaza, and you will see a tall white obelisk dedicated to one of King's important mentors and personal friends, Howard Thurman. A bust of Thurman and selected quotes from his many writings appear on and around the monument. To the left of the obelisk, under the ground-level inscriptions, are interred the ashes of Thurman and his wife, Sue Bailey Thurman (a 1920 graduate of Spelman Seminary).

Thurman attended Morehouse College and graduated in 1923. At Morehouse he was a classmate and friend of Martin Luther King, Sr. The two often had dinner together in the King home on Auburn Avenue. In 1936 Thurman and his wife, Sue Bailey

The Greatest Speech of the 20th Century
"I HAVE A DREAM"

Martin Luther King, Jr. '48
August 28, 1963
The Lincoln Memorial
Washington, D.C.

Bronze Plaque Engraved with Text of "I Have a Dream"

Thurman, traveled to India with Edward and
Phenola Carroll. While in India, the four met with
Gandhi and discussed with him ways to transplant
his nonviolent tactics to the United States to fight
segregation.

In 1953, during his final year of study for his
Ph.D. in theology at Boston University, Martin
Luther King, Jr., met Thurman. At the time,
Thurman was dean of the Marsh Chapel (the first
black to hold that position at any major university).
The two became close friends, and Thurman became
a mentor to King, sharing with him what he had
learned about nonviolent resistance from Gandhi.
As often as he could, King listened to Thurman
preach in Marsh Chapel and read Thurman's
writings about nonviolence. During the last decade
of King's life, the two exchanged frequent letters.

Of all of Thurman's books, one, in
particular, influenced King's thinking and
actions—Thurman's 1949 book, Jesus
and the Disinherited.[43] As many of King's
co-workers recall, King carried this book
with him during the Montgomery
bus boycott and other civil rights
campaigns. It is easy to understand
why King found Thurman's thin

Howard Thurman

volume so inspiring. Thurman described Jesus as a "poor Jew" and a social revolutionary and discussed the similarity between the social position of Jesus in Palestine and that of the vast majority of African Americans in the United States in the 1940s. Thurman declared that the similarity is "obvious to anyone who tarries long over the facts.… It is the similarity of a social climate at the point of a denial of full citizenship."[44]

Howard Thurman Obelisk

Clark Atlanta University/ Morehouse College Quadrangle

223 James P. Brawley Dr., SW

A short distance north of the King Chapel is the quadrangle shared by Morehouse College and Clark Atlanta University. This large, open space was the location of a number of significant civil rights-related activities. The south end of the quadrangle was the gathering place and starting point for many of the demonstrations and marches of the 1960s. In 2000, on the occasion of the fortieth anniversary of the first sit-in, a group of former AUC students erected a small plaque on the lawn in front of the Trevor Arnett building.

The north end of the quadrangle is also a sacred spot, for it was there, on April 9, 1968, that 50,000 mourners gathered to honor Dr. King on the afternoon of his funeral. The speakers for the occasion addressed the crowd from the steps of Atlanta University's Harkness Hall. Benjamin Mays, president of Morehouse, eulogized his friend and former student:

Fortieth Anniversary Plaque

> *To be honored by being requested to give the Eulogy at the funeral of Dr. Martin Luther King, Jr., is like being asked to eulogize a deceased son—so close and so precious was he to me. Our friendship goes back to his student days at Morehouse College.... Fate has decreed that I eulogize him. I wish it might have been otherwise, for, after all, I am three score years and ten and Martin Luther is dead at thirty-nine.*

Harkness Hall, Clark Atlanta University

On February 23, 1968, six weeks before his death, King participated in the one hundredth anniversary celebration of the birth of W. E. B. Du Bois at Carnegie Hall in New York. An early civil rights giant, Du Bois twice taught at Atlanta University, the first time from 1898–1910 and the second time from 1934–44. In his tribute to Du Bois, King singled out the importance of Du Bois's book, *Black Reconstruction in America*, which was published in 1935 while Du Bois was at Atlanta University.

W. E. B. Du Bois's Contributions to Civil Rights While on the Faculty of Atlanta University

BOOKS *The Philadelphia Negro* (1899), *The Souls of Black Folk* (1903), *John Brown* (1909), *The Quest of the Silver Fleece* (1911), *Black Reconstruction in America* (1935), *and Dusk of Dawn* (1940).

OTHER ACCOMPLISHMENTS Founded The Niagra Movement (1905), the National Association for the Advancement of Colored People (NAACP) (1909), and the journal *Phylon* (1940).

Du Bois left Atlanta during the summer of 1944, just a few weeks before King arrived as a freshman at Morehouse College. The two probably never met in Atlanta or elsewhere, but certainly King was influenced by Du Bois in the development of his own civil rights thinking and actions.

As you stand in front of Harkness Hall, note the cluster of shrubbery in front of and slightly south of the building. If you look behind the bushes, you will see a flat memorial stone marking the grave of John

Dr. King's casket on the steps of Harkness Hall. Jesse Jackson is second from the right.

Hope (1868–1936), the first African-American president of Morehouse College. Hope served as president from 1906–1931 and also as president of Atlanta University from 1929–1936. His wife, Lugenia Burns Hope (1871–1947), is not buried beside him. She requested that her ashes be scattered over the campus from the tower of Graves Hall.

After visiting Harkness Hall and the John Hope gravesite, walk to the building at the far west end of the quadrangle. You again will be on the campus of Morehouse College. The building, Graves Hall, was built in 1889 and is the oldest building on the Morehouse campus.

Note the statue in front of Graves Hall. The statue, sculpted by Edward J. Dwight, is of Benjamin E. Mays, a man who provided outstanding leadership and service as a teacher, preacher, mentor, scholar, author, and leader in the civil rights movement.

More specifically, Mays is the man Martin Luther King, Jr., knew as his spiritual mentor and intellectual father.

The youngest of eight children, Mays was born on August 1, 1894, near Epworth, South Carolina, to Louvenia Carter and Hezekiah Mays, tenant farmers and former slaves. However, the young Mays overcame his lowly background and, in 1920, graduated Phi Beta Kappa from Bates College in Maine. After a few semesters at the University of Chicago, he came to Atlanta to serve as the pastor of Shiloh Baptist Church (1921–1923). Also, during this time, 1921 to 1924, he taught

Benjamin E. Mays Statue, Graves Hall

mathematics and was the debate coach at Morehouse College. In 1924, he left Morehouse to attend the University of Chicago Divinity School, where he earned a master's degree in 1925 and a PhD in 1935.

From 1934 to 1940, Mays served as dean of the School of Religion at Howard University in Washington, DC. In 1940, he was appointed president of Morehouse College, a position he held until 1967. During his twenty-seven-year tenure, Dr. Mays deeply inspired his students, including Martin Luther King, Jr., who attended Morehouse from 1944–1948. Every Tuesday morning, Dr. Mays addressed the students in the chapel in Sale Hall and challenged them to excel in scholarship and service. During these sessions, he also shared with them details of his trip to India in 1936 and about his lengthy conversation with Mahatma Gandhi.

Upon retirement from Morehouse, Mays served for eleven years (1970–1981) as president of the Atlanta Board of Education. He died in 1984. His wife, Sadie Gray, a teacher and social worker whom he had married in 1926, preceded him in death. She died in 1969.

Throughout his career, Mays received fifty-six honorary degrees, including one from Columbia University awarded posthumously. He published nearly two thousand articles and nine books, including his acclaimed autobiography, *Born to Rebel* (New York: Scribner's, 1971).

The Mays memorial, with its statue and crypt, was dedicated in 1995. Buried beneath the statue is a time capsule to be opened in 2095.

Benjamin E. Mays (1894–1984) and Sadie Gray Mays (1900–1969) now rest in the double crypt in the shadow of Dr. Mays's statue in front of Graves Hall.

Crypt of Benjamin E. Mays and Sadie Gray Mays

Robert W. Woodruff Library
Atlanta University Center

111 James P. Brawley Dr., SW

www.auctr.edu

About two blocks north of the Clark Atlanta University/Morehouse College campus quadrangle on Brawley Drive stands the Robert W. Woodruff Library, the library shared by all the institutions in the Atlanta University Center. The library's Archives and Special Collections division, located on the second level, houses the library's extensive African-American collection as well as many materials related to the civil rights movement, including correspondence, reports, photographs, and slides.

In June 2006, Morehouse College, in cooperation with Mayor Shirley Franklin and other civic, education and business leaders, purchased more than 7,000 notes, speeches, sermons and other documents of Martin Luther King, Jr., from the King estate for $32 million. The papers and documents were written and collected by King from 1946 until his death in 1968 and include copies of his "I Have A Dream" speech, his "Letter from Birmingham Jail," and his 1964 Nobel Peace prize acceptance speech, as well as nearly one hundred handwritten sermons. The collection initially will be placed in the archives at the Woodruff Library at the Atlanta University Center. Plans under discussion include eventually housing the collection in a new archives at Morehouse College or in the new Center for Civil and Human Rights to be opened in downtown Atlanta in 2010.

Woodruff Library, Atlanta University Center

In June 2007, the investment bank Goldman Sachs donated $2 million to Morehouse to endow the Goldman Sachs Leadership Chair in Civil and Human Rights. The chair holder ultimately will be director of the Morehouse College Martin Luther King, Jr., Collection.

In November 2007, Atlanta University Center's Woodruff Library received a $400,000 grant from the Andrew W. Mellon Foundation to complete processing the papers and to develop a digital search engine for the King Collection.

Rush Memorial Congregational Church

150 James P. Brawley Dr., SW (formerly Chestnut St.)

During the 1960s, the students of the Atlanta University Center used donated space in this church as the headquarters for their organization, the Committee On Appeal for Human Rights

Rush Memorial Congregational Church

(COAHR). The church was convenient to all the campuses in the AUC. The pastor of the church at the time, the Reverend Joseph E. Boone, invited the students to use several rooms in the church after they no longer were able to use Sage Hall at Morehouse for their offices. The invitation cost the church some members who left because they disagreed with the students' activities.

COAHR was a very efficiently structured organization led by two co-chairs, usually a male and a female. Other designated officers included an executive officer (known as le Commandante), a deputy chief of operations, a senior intelligence officer, field and area commanders, a secretary, and a treasurer.

Reports from the field and area commanders were sent by radio and telephone to the movement headquarters at Rush Memorial. The reports were then typed, dated, and placed on the desk of le

Commandante. Duplicates were placed on the headquarters' bulletin board so students could stay abreast of what was happening downtown.

A plaque with information about the students' organization has been placed on a historic marker in front of the church.

Warren Memorial United Methodist Church

181 Joseph Lowery Blvd., SW (formerly Ashby St.)

www.warrenmemorial.org

Early in March 1960, students, representatives from the black community, and business leaders held a series of meetings downtown to discuss plans for the desegregation of the city's lunch counters and business establishments. An agreement was finally reached late Sunday night, March 6, and made public the following day. Merchants throughout the city responded favorably to the plan. The reaction from the black community—including the students who had sacrificed so much and who had spent so many days in jail—was less favorable; many thought the desegregation plans were too moderate and the time line for implementation too slow.

Because of the harsh criticisms of the agreement, the negotiators arranged for a public meeting at the Warren Memorial United Methodist Church on March 10. More than two thousand people attended, approximately two-thirds of whom were students. Loud-speakers were set up outside to accommodate the overflow crowd.

Warren Memorial United Methodist Church

One of the speakers at the meeting who supported the agreement was Martin Luther King, Sr. The applause that greeted him was subdued. Then one of the students yelled "Sellout!" After an awkward silence, King, Sr., began to speak. He spoke slowly, but deliberately: "By your saying I've sold out bothers me very little.… If you want the little place I have you can have it. I'm tired, as tired as I can be.… Now God bless you, and let's keep working together for the good of all of us."[45]

As the meeting continued, the crowd grew more restless, and members of the younger generation began to attack the members of the older generation for their more conservative approach to social change. In this boisterous and turbulent atmosphere, the moderator asked Martin Luther King, Jr., to speak. Slowly, King approached the pulpit and turned to face an angry, but—for the moment— hushed crowd: "We must honestly say to Atlanta that time is running out. If some concrete changes for good are not made soon, Negro leaders of the city will find it impossible to convince the masses of Negroes of the good faith of the negotiations presently taking place.... Atlanta needs an Amos to cry out, 'Let justice roll down like waters and right-eousness like a mighty stream.' Atlanta needs another Jefferson to scratch across the pages of history words lifted to cosmic proportions: 'We hold these truths to be self-evident that all men are created equal.'"[46]

The younger King, like his father, no doubt supported the negotiations. However, King, Jr., whose age bridged the generations and who had gained the respect of the younger generation, was able to function as an effective mediator.

By the time King had finished speaking, the anger among the younger generation was dissipated and the audience was quieted. The opposition to the agreement had been silenced.

Martin Luther King, Jr. Drive
(Formerly Hunter Street)

DIRECTIONS BY CAR FROM THE NORTH Take I-75/85 south to Martin Luther King, Jr. Dr. (Exit 248A). Go west on Martin Luther King, Jr. Dr. 0.5 mile until you come to the Sam Nunn Atlanta Federal Center at the northwest corner of Martin Luther King, Jr. Drive and Forsyth Street. Park in one of the many parking lots near the center.

DIRECTIONS BY CAR FROM THE SOUTH Take I-75/85 north to Edgewood Avenue (Exit 248B). Turn left on Edgewood. Go under the underpass, turn left onto I-75/85 south, and follow the directions above.

DIRECTIONS BY MARTA Take any of the train or bus lines to the Five Points Station (M). Exit the station on the Forsyth Street side and walk one block south to the Sam Nunn Atlanta Federal Center at 61 Forsyth Street. After visiting the center, exit, turn right and walk a half block to Martin Luther King, Jr. Dr. to continue the tour. Also, the No. 3 bus leaves from the Five Points train station (M) and runs along Martin Luther King, Jr. Dr.

SACRED PLACES M.L.K. JR. DRIVE

A Mural, "Sitting Down at Rich's", Lobby of Sam Nunn Atlanta Federal Center, *Corner of Spring and MLK, Jr. Dr.*

B Herndon Home, *587 University Place*

C Martin Luther King, Jr. Family Residence, *234 Sunset Ave.*

D Old West Hunter Street Baptist Church, *775 MLK, Jr. Dr.*

E Student Nonviolent Coordinating Committee (SNCC) Office, *6-8 1/2 Raymond St.*

F Old Paschal's Restaurant, *830 MLK, Jr. Dr.*

G Frazier's Café Society (now Sweet Pie 'n' Buy Restaurant), *880 MLK, Jr. Dr.*

H Atlanta Inquirer Office, *947 MLK, Jr. Dr.*

I Booker T. Washington High School, *45 Whitehouse Dr.*

Vine City Neighborhood

Tour 3 begins with a visit to the Sitting Down at Rich's mural in the lobby of the Sam Nunn Atlanta Federal Center near downtown Atlanta and then continues west on Martin Luther King., Jr. Drive for seven or eight blocks.

In the 1940s and 1950s, Martin Luther King Jr., Drive west of Northside Drive (then known as West Hunter Street) was the second major Atlanta avenue of black businesses, residences, and social institutions. The first, of course, was Auburn Avenue whose illustrious history and developments are highlighted in Tour 1. Auburn Avenue reached its zenith in the 1920s and 30s but in the following decades the vitality of "Sweet Auburn" shifted to West Hunter Street. Much of the development of West Hunter was driven by business interests but also by the influences from the nearby working-class neighborhood of Vine City and nearby middle-class Atlanta University Center complex. **(SEE TOUR 2 FOR DETAILS ABOUT THE ATLANTA UNIVERSITY CENTER.)**

After you cross over Northside Dr., continue for one block and look to your left and you will see two educational institutions that were or are affiliated with the Atlanta University Center consortium. The first, Morris Brown College, is no longer a part of the consortium because it lost its accreditation. The second, immediately west of Morris Brown, is the Interdenominational Theological Center (ITC) and is one of the four institutions that currently make up the Atlanta University Center.

As you pass Morris Brown College and continue westward, note the eleven historic markers on both sides of Martin Luther King, Jr. Dr. Nine of the markers are on pedestals standing on the sidewalk; two are attached to the walls of buildings.

The markers provide information about significant

buildings, people, and events that were a part of Martin Luther King, Jr. Drive's memorable social, economic, and civil rights past.

Mural, "Sitting Down at Rich's"
Lobby of Sam Nunn Atlanta Federal Center

61 Forsyth St., SW (Corner of Spring and MLK, Jr. Dr.)
(formerly Rich's Department Store)

Rich's department store was the target of many of the students' sit-in actions as early as the spring of 1960. In the summer of 1960, students organized sit-ins at Rich's restaurants and later organized a boycott of the store. The best known of their demonstrations occurred October 19, 1960, when Martin Luther King, Jr., joined the students at the Magnolia Tea Room on the sixth floor. Dr. King and the students were arrested.

In the mid-1990s, part of Rich's was razed and replaced by the Sam Nunn Atlanta Federal Center

Arrest at Rich's, October 19, 1960

"Sitting Down at Rich's" Mural

(completed in two phases in 1996 and 1998).
Mounted on a wall of the main lobby of the new
center is a large mural memorializing significant
events in Rich's history, including the sit-in on
October 19, 1960, when King was arrested.
Designed by Mike Mandel and titled Sitting Down
At Rich's, the mural is constructed of one-inch-
square colored porcelain and glass mosaic tiles. The
mural, installed in January and February 2000,
begins on a corridor wall leading to the cafeteria,
wraps around that wall into the main lobby, and
extends up the stairs to the second floor. To design
the centerpiece of the mural, Mandel copied an
image from an Associated Press photograph
published on the front page of the Atlanta
Constitution on October 20, 1960. This part of the
mural, which directly faces

the main lobby of the Federal Center, depicts four individuals arrested at Rich's during the sit-in on October 19. Shown left to right on the 30' x 30' mural are Lonnie King, Morehouse College student leader; Marilyn Pryce, Spelman sophomore; Martin Luther King, Jr.; and Ida Rose McCree, Spelman sophomore, carrying a sign that reads "WE WANT TO SIT DOWN LIKE EVERYONE ELSE." Mounted on the wall of the corridor leading to the cafeteria are several 8-inch by 10-inch porcelain tiles of photographs taken on the day of the sit-in. One shows the original Associated Press photograph from which the mural centerpiece was designed. Another depicts two Spelman students, Marilyn Pryce and Blondean Orbert, exiting Rich's with Lonnie King and Martin Luther King, Jr. The four, accompanied by Atlanta Police captain R. E. Little, are on their way to jail where they were joined by forty-eight other students arrested with them on the same day.

Vine City Neighborhood

Northside Dr. and Martin Luther King, Jr. Dr., NW

Vine City is one of the oldest neighborhoods in Atlanta. Before the Civil War it was settled by both blacks and whites, but by the early twentieth century it had developed into a stable black residential area for working-, middle-, and upper-class black families. Vine City's residents have included Alonzo Herndon, founder of the Atlanta Life Insurance Company; Horace Mann Bond, professor of Education at Atlanta University and father of civil rights leader Julian Bond; Maynard Jackson, three-term Atlanta mayor (1974–78, 1978–82, and 1990–94); and Martin Luther King, Jr., and family.

Beginning in the 1950s, Vine City, like other inner-city black neighborhoods, changed rapidly and radically. With a few exceptions (such as the Kings), most middle-class and upper-class families left Vine City and moved to the suburbs. At the same time, housing shifted from resident owners to absentee landlords. Consequently, within the span of a few years, Vine City changed from a neighborhood of stable and respected families to a neighborhood inflicted with all the classic problems of urban slums: unemployment, deteriorating housing, crime, poor schools, inadequate public services, powerlessness, and political apathy.

SNCC's offices were located only a few blocks from Vine City, and the staff members were aware of the changes in the neighborhood. With hopes of reversing the neighborhood's deteriorating conditions and of empowering the neighborhood's residents, a group of SNCC staff organized the Atlanta Project in early 1966.

The members of the Atlanta Project approached their work in Vine City with a "blacks-only" interpretation of Black Power. They expected and encouraged white SNCC activists to organize in their own white communities.

Former Spelman student, Gwen Robinson, joined the Atlanta Project in 1966, after having served for nearly two years as director of SNCC's Laurel, Mississippi project, both during and after the 1964 Mississippi Freedom Summer. In a 1998 interview, Gwen recalled that the organizers of the Atlanta Project thought that the whites within SNCC should organize their own communities. "We were saying that the problem of racism lies in the white community and while it is wonderful for all of us to be here together in the black community, there is no way that I, as a black person, can organize in the white community. So who is going to do it? You have to go do it and we meet down the road. This was the vision that those of us in the Atlanta Project had."[47]

Today, Vine City is still struggling, although some new housing has been built and other improvements have been made. However, the problems were compounded when the Georgia Dome was built across Northside Drive; the noise and traffic make Vine City a less attractive place to live.

Herndon Home

587 University Place, NW

www.nps.gov/nr/travel/atlanta/her.htm

This house, built by black artisans, was designed by Alonzo and Adrienne (McNeil) Herndon. The Herndons, who married in 1893, were both prominent members of Atlanta's upper-class black community. Accumulating wealth from his three downtown barbershops and real estate investments, Alonzo became Atlanta's first black millionaire. In 1905 he purchased the Atlanta Protective and Benevolent Association for $140, which he reorganized into the Atlanta Life Insurance Company. Today, Atlanta Life (as it now known) is the largest black-owned insurance company in the United States. **(SEE TOUR 1 FOR MORE DETAILS AND PHOTOGRAPHS OF THE ATLANTA LIFE INSURANCE COMPANY.)**

SACRED PLACES M.L.K. JR. DRIVE

Adrienne joined the Atlanta University faculty in 1895, becoming one of only three African Americans on the faculty (the other two were W. E. B. Du Bois and George Towns). Together, the young couple designed the house, but tragically, just one week before the house was completed, Adrienne died of Addison's disease.

After Adrienne's untimely death, Alonzo married Jessie Gillespie and together the new couple and Alonzo and Adrienne's son, Norris, became the residents of the house.

The National Park Service website provides the following description of the architecture of the house:

Herndon Home

> *The Herndon home is a two-story, 15-room Beaux Arts mansion built by local black craftsmen. The formally composed building is constructed with multi-colored brick, and features a two-story entry portico supported by Corinthian columns. One-story porches to each side of the building echo this theme in brick piers and wooden capitals. An elliptical fanlight over the main entrance and the balustrade above the full entablature of the building's cornice add a distinctly Georgian Revival flavor to this imposing residence.[48]*

Following Alonzo's death in 1927, the Herndon's son, Norris, moved into the house. Norris envisioned the house as a museum in honor of his parents. On his many trips to Europe, he collected decorative arts and furnishings for the house, many of which are still in the house today. Norris died in 1977.

Tours are available Monday through Friday, 10:00–4:00, and on Saturday by appointment. Admission is $5 for adults and $3 for children. Check the Herndon Home Web site (or call 404-581-9813 for more information.

Martin Luther King, Jr., Family Residence

234 Sunset Ave., NW

In early 1965, Martin Luther King, Jr., Coretta, and their four children moved into a house on the high ground on the west side of Vine City. They could have lived in a more prestigious neighborhood, but

King Family Residence

Martin and Coretta chose to live and raise their children in this modest, working-class neighborhood.

The family was living here when Martin was assassinated in 1968. Until his death, King maintained a basement study, and he left behind hundreds of books and thousands of papers containing his sermons, speeches, and correspondence. For decades, the materials remained undisturbed in the basement study. Then, a few years ago, the King family incorporated these materials with an assortment of King's other books and papers and offered them for sale. In June 2006, Morehouse College and the City of Atlanta purchased the collection of more than 7,000 papers and books from the King estate for $32 million. The Sunset Avenue materials make up a large portion of the collection they purchased.

In 2003, Mrs. King moved out of the house on Sunset Avenue and into two thirty-ninth-floor condominium units (donated by Oprah Winfrey) in Buckhead in North Atlanta. Mrs. King died three years later, on January 30, 2006. In 2008, the house on Sunset Avenue was still owned by the King estate.

D

Old West Hunter Street Baptist Church

775 Martin Luther King, Jr. Dr., NW

In 1961, Ralph David Abernathy resigned as pastor of First Baptist Church in Montgomery, Alabama, and moved to Atlanta to become the pastor of West Hunter Street Baptist Church. As pastor of the church and as secretary-treasurer of the Southern Christian Leadership Conference (SCLC), he continued his leadership in the civil rights movement and worked as second-in-command to Martin Luther King, Jr. After King's death in 1968, Abernathy replaced him as president of SCLC.

At West Hunter, Abernathy continued to preach and practice the progressive message of his predecessor, the Reverend A. Franklin Fisher, who was one of the ministers arrested in the Triple L (Law, Love and Liberation) bus desegregation campaign of 1957. **(SEE THE "BRIEF HISTORY OF THE CIVIL RIGHTS MOVEMENT IN ATLANTA" FOR MORE DETAILS ABOUT THE TRIPLE L MOVEMENT.)**

Located only a few blocks from the Atlanta University Center, West Hunter was a favorite church for students. Listening to Abernathy's sermons inspired them to get involved in the civil rights movement and to organize actions for desegregation and social change.

In 1973, Abernathy and his congregation moved to 1040 Ralph David Abernathy Boulevard SW (formerly Gordon Street) in the West End neighborhood. Abernathy continued to minister there until shortly before his death on April 17, 1990. He is entombed in Lincoln Cemetery in West Atlanta. The inscription on his mausoleum reads "I tried." His

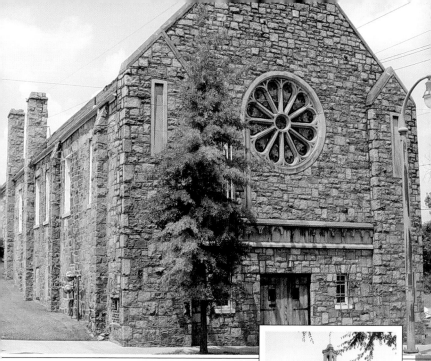

Old West Hunter Baptist Church

autobiography, And the Walls Came Tumbling Down, was published in 1989.

Following the move of the West Hunter congregation to West End, the building on Hunter Street was used for a number of years by the Grace Covenant Baptist Church. Today the building stands empty and is in need of repair. However, in early 2008, the Abernathy family announced plans to purchase the building and to turn it into the Ralph David Abernathy Center for Civil Rights History and Wax Museum.

Current West Hunter Baptist Church, 1040 Ralph David Abernathy Blvd., SW

Student Nonviolent Coordinating Committee (SNCC) Office

6–8½ Raymond Street, NW (Marx building)

The Student Nonviolent Coordinating Committee (SNCC) was founded at a meeting convened by the Southern Christian Leadership Conference (SCLC) at Shaw University in Raleigh, North Carolina, in the spring of 1960. SCLC offered the fledgling organization a "windowless cubicle" in the corner of its office at 208 Auburn Avenue. After a short stay, SNCC moved to 197½ Auburn, and then to 6 Raymond Street in the spring of 1962. The group soon outgrew the 6 Raymond Street office and expanded to 8½ Raymond Street next door.

During the Easter break of 1962, a group of students and their professor from Ohio Wesleyan University visited the SNCC office at 197½ Auburn Avenue. One of the students, Mary King, later wrote about their visit with vivid detail:

> [We] walked gingerly up the stairs into the grimy office wondering what the nerve center of the black sit-in movement would look like. Papers were strewn across every desk with unstudied abandon. Telephones were ringing, wastebaskets bulged with trash, and file-cabinet drawers gaped open. A mimeograph machine monotonously whooshed paper through its rollers in the background, and a radio somewhere thumped a heavy beat. The floors looked as if they had not been scrubbed since installation, and the windows were opaque with dust.[49]

SNCC Office

Mary King joined SNCC in June 1963 and worked in the Raymond Street office as the assistant to SNCC's press secretary, Julian Bond. She later described the Raymond Street office as a "ramshackle mint-green two-story building…above a tailor shop." Close by was Alex's Barbecue Heaven. Mary reported that when the wind was blowing in their direction, smoke from Alex's barbecue pit would waft through their open office windows. "When the scent was particularly pungent, our small office building would temporarily empty as SNCC staff people trickled out to bring back barbecued spareribs or chicken to their desks and satisfy the yearning stimulated by the piquant smell."[50]

During the years the office was on Raymond Street, many students from the nearby Atlanta University Center volunteered to work in the office and joined the picket lines and demonstrations that the SNCC staff organized.

In May 1965, SNCC moved its office from Raymond Street to 360 Nelson Street. Five year later, financially bankrupt and in political disarray, the organization closed its office and ceased operation.

The most effective years of SNCC were from 1960–1965. During those years, SNCC had an organizational structure that was equalitarian, consensus-building, and anti-hierarchical, and an ideology that espoused inclusion and cooperation among social classes and between blacks and whites. After 1965, however, SNCC's organizational structure became more and more hierarchical and centralized, and a serious rift developed between black and white SNCC activists.

The changes were both a cause and an effect of the election of Stokely Carmichael as SNCC chair in May 1966. The emphasis on black nationalism and black power and the weakening of the organization's commitment to nonviolence that came with Carmichael's chairmanship alienated many liberal whites and conservative blacks who, in response, ceased providing financial support for the beleaguered organization.

Today, The Raymond Street office building has been replaced by a Publix supermarket, which is part of a "new urbanism" development known as Historic Westside Village. The Nelson Street office building was torn down in 2006.

Old Paschal's Restaurant

830 Martin Luther King, Jr. Dr., NW

www.paschalsrestaurant.net/history.htm

Paschal's was founded as a sandwich shop by brothers Robert and James Paschal in 1947. As business grew, they expanded the sandwich shop and opened a motel and restaurant in 1959. One year later they added a nightclub, La Carousel, on the lower level. Among the luminaries who performed at the nightclub were Ramsey Lewis, Cannonball Adderly, Joe Williams, Dizzy Gillespie, and Aretha Franklin.

During the 1960s, Paschal's was known as the "kitchen of the civil rights movement."[51] Paschal's restaurant was one of the few places in Atlanta where black and white civil rights leaders and students could meet to plan for demonstrations and to recover after days and nights on the picket line or in jail. For example, it was here that Martin Luther King, Jr., and his lieutenants planned the Selma-to-Montgomery march in 1965 and the Poor People's Campaign in the spring of 1968 (shortly before King's death). In 2005, King's widow, Coretta Scott King, declared that "Paschal's is as important a historical site for the American civil rights movement as Boston's Faneuil Hall is to the American Revolution."[52] And the longtime president of the

Old Paschal's Restaurant

Southern Christian Leadership Conference, the Reverend Joseph Lowery, said that "the history of the movement was closely aligned with the history of this old meeting place."[53]

In 1996 Clark Atlanta University purchased the old establishment and for a few years used the motel as a dormitory. However, the university consistently lost money and after a few years announced plans to tear down both the motel and restaurant. The restaurant served its last meal on July 28, 2003.

An outcry of protest followed the university's announcement that they planned to raze the historic buildings. Several plans to save the restaurant as a historic site have been generated. As of August 2008, both buildings are still standing, although rapidly deteriorating.

In 2002, James Paschal, 79, and Herman Russell, Sr., 71, opened a new inn and restaurant known as "Paschal's at Castleberry Hill" at 180 Northside Drive.

Frazier's Café Society
(Now Food for Life Supreme Restaurant)

Evelyn Jones Frazier, a pioneer westside Atlanta businesswoman, and her husband, Luther, opened Frazier's in 1946. Their restaurant remained one of Atlanta's most popular meeting places for African Americans for more than thirty years. Its banquet room, named "The Graham Jackson Room," in honor of Atlanta's well-known musician, hosted many fundraisers and meetings for local civic and political activities.

Along with Paschal's, Frazier's was a frequent meeting place for civil rights workers in the 1960s. This was especially true for the young staff and volunteers of SNCC who often chose Frazier's over Paschal's for their meeting place.

On the afternoon and evening of Saturday, March 6, 1965, SNCC held a very important meeting here.

Former Frazier's Café

Their agenda was to decide if SNCC would participate in the Selma-to-Montgomery march scheduled for the following day. The meeting was chaired by John Lewis. Also present were Jim Forman, Marion Barry, Courtland Cox, Ivanhoe Donaldson, Julian Bond, Bob Mants, Silas Norman, Wilson Brown, Judy Richardson, and Ruby Doris Smith Robinson.

The debate went on for hours, long after day had turned to night. A consensus developed that SNCC should not participate in the march, but John Lewis told the group that he felt that it was up to the people of Selma to decide whether or not to march, and that SNCC needed to support them, whatever their decision. "If they wanted to march, we should march with them," he said. Then just before midnight, he made a final statement: "I'm a native Alabamian. I grew up in Alabama. I feel a deep kinship with the people there on a lot of levels. You know I've been to Selma many, many times. I've been arrested there. I've been jailed there. If these people want to march, I'm going to march with them."[54]

The next day in Selma, John and fellow activist Hosea Williams were chosen to lead a march to Montgomery. A group of five hundred marchers fell in line behind the two leaders as they moved out of Selma and toward the Edmund Pettus Bridge. When they reached the far side of the bridge, the marchers were brutally attacked by the sheriff and his posse. Dozens, including John, were seriously injured.

The date of the march, March 7, 1965, has been recorded in the annals of civil rights history as a day of infamy. It will always be remembered as "Bloody Sunday."

Atlanta Inquirer Office

947 Martin Luther King, Jr. Dr., NW

www.atlinq.com

The editors of the Atlanta Daily World, Atlanta's black newspaper since 1928, often refused to publish information about the civil rights movement or, if they did, they were critical of what the participants were doing. So a group of students and faculty from the Atlanta University Center decided to start their own newspaper. They named it the Atlanta Inquirer and published the first issue on July 31, 1960. Through the remaining years of the movement, the paper provided detailed coverage of the students' activities in Atlanta and elsewhere. The paper is still in publication as a weekly.

In a storage room in back of the newspaper's offices, several filing cabinets contain folders and photographs collected by the newspaper's staff and journalists over the years. Many of the materials and photographs deal with civil rights activities in Atlanta and elsewhere.

Atlanta Inquirer Office

129

SACRED PLACES M.L.K., JR. DRIVE

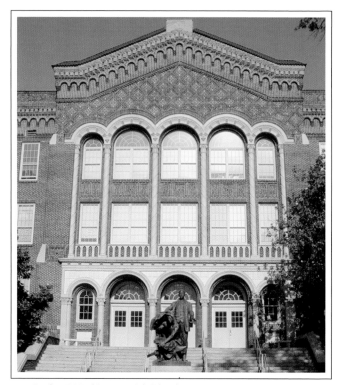

Booker T. Washington High School

Booker T. Washington High School

45 Whitehouse Dr., SW

www.apskids.org/washington

Named for the early twentieth-century black educator, Washington High School opened in 1924 with 1565 students and 32 teachers. It was not just the first high school built for African Americans in Atlanta; it was, in fact, the first in the state of Georgia. Designed by Atlanta-born architect Eugene C. Waehendorff, the building incorporates Medieval and Byzantine elements, including the dramatic entrance with five arches in two tiers.

Adorning a wall of the central corridor are seven murals depicting the dignity of labor painted by former student Wilmer Jennings. Outside, in front of the main entrance, is a replica of the original Booker T. Washington bronze statue on the campus of Tuskegee University in Tuskegee, Alabama. The statue, sculpted by Charles Keek, shows Washington pulling back the veil of ignorance from the head of an uneducated black man. The liberated man is holding a large book in his lap and by his side is a plow. At the base of the statue is the following inscription: "He lifted the veil of ignorance from his people and pointed the way to progress through education and industry."

Martin Luther King, Jr., attended Washington High School as a sophomore and junior, from 1942–1944. The two previous years, 1940–1942, he was a student at the Atlanta University Laboratory School, attending classes in Giles Hall on the campus of Spelman College. However, when he transferred from the Laboratory School to Washington High School, he skipped ninth grade. And, then in his senior year, he took and passed a college entrance exam, which allowed him to skip twelfth grade and enter Morehouse College as a freshman in 1944. He was fifteen years old.

King Rode Segregated School Bus
to Washington High School

I went to high school on the other side of town—to
Booker T. Washington High School. I had to get the bus in
what was known as the Fourth Ward and ride over to the
West Side. In those days, rigid patterns of segregation
existed on the buses, so that Negroes had to sit in the
backs of buses.… I would end up having to go to the
back of that bus with my body, but every time I got on
that bus I left my mind up in the front seat. And I said to
myself, "One of these days, I'm going to put my body up
there where my mind is."[55]

The school is not open to the public. You may
freely view the outside sites but would need special
permission to visit inside the school building.

Four Scattered Sites

The four sites on Tour 4, as the name suggests, are scattered across the city. In fact, one site is located in each of the four quadrants of the city. These sites can be visited most conveniently by car, but they can also be reached by public transportation. Directions to each site are given at the beginning of the discussion of each site.

"The Bridge"
Sculpture honoring John Lewis

Corner of Freedom Parkway
and Ponce de Leon Ave., NE

DIRECTIONS BY CAR Take I-75/85 north or south to Freedom Parkway (Exit 248C). Travel east 1.6 miles to the dead end of Freedom Parkway at Ponce de Leon Ave. The sculpture is at the southeast corner of the intersection.

DIRECTIONS BY MARTA Take any MARTA train to the Five Points Station (M). Then, take the 16 Noble bus to the Carter Center and walk two blocks north to "The Bridge" sculpture.

The forty-two-foot-long sculpture, "The Bridge," honors the many civil rights achievements of Congressman John Lewis. The sculptor, Thornton Dial, was inspired to create the work by Lewis's march across the Edmund Pettus Bridge in Selma, Alabama, on March 7, 1965.

In his autobiography, Walking with the Wind, John describes what occurred when the marchers reached the far side of the Edmund Pettus bridge on that fateful day:

> The troopers and possemen swept forward as one, like a human wave, a blur of blue shirts and billy clubs and bullwhips.... I remember how vivid the sounds were as the troopers rushed toward us—the clunk of the troopers' heavy boots, the whoops of rebel yells from the white onlookers, the clip-clop of horses' hooves hitting the hard asphalt of the highway.... I heard something that sounded like gunshots. And then a cloud of smoke rose all around us. Tear gas." [56]

John was hit over the head and suffered a fractured skull. Dazed and bleeding, he somehow managed to stumble back to Brown Chapel. There gathered all around the church were dozens of others who had been wounded.

Made of castoff objects such as tires, iron rods, strips of corrugated metal, pipes and decorative wrought iron, the multi-figured sculpture not only symbolizes the "Bloody Sunday" march but the many other bridges Lewis crossed during his years as civil rights leader, Atlanta city councilman, and US congressman.

The sculpture was dedicated on September 9, 2005. In his remarks at the dedication ceremony,

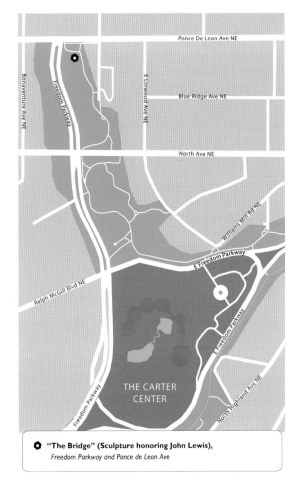

● **"The Bridge" (Sculpture honoring John Lewis),**
Freedom Parkway and Ponce de Leon Ave

Dial said that the hardest kind of bridges to build are bridges in our minds and hearts, "bridges that enable us to move from one state of mind to another." Yet, Dial continued, Lewis has lived his entire life trying to construct those kinds of bridges: "Whether by organizing students in opposition to Jim Crow racism in Nashville, Tennessee, or by challenging his colleagues to re-set their moral compasses on the House floor in Washington, DC, or by literally

"The Bridge"

walking across the Edmund Pettus Bridge one bloody Sunday morning in 1965."[57]

After visiting "The Bridge," we suggest you visit the Carter Center Museum, located just two blocks south of the Lewis Memorial, at 1 Copenhill Ave., NE (www.cartercenter.org; 404-331-3900)

Pickrick Restaurant

881 Hemphill Ave., NW
(formerly 891 Hemphill Ave. NW)

DIRECTIONS BY CAR Take I-75/85 north or south to the 10th St./14th exit (Exit 250). Travel west on 10th Street 0.7 mile to Hemphill Ave. Turn left on Hemphill and go 0.1 mile to 881 Hemphill on your left.

Take the north line train to the Midtown station (N4). Take the No. 37 bus west on 10th St. to Hemphill Ave. Walk two blocks south to 881 Hemphill.

The Pickrick Restaurant, located near Georgia Institute of Technology, was owned and operated from 1947 to 1965 by Lester Maddox. Famous for its fried chicken, the restaurant quickly became popular and by the late 1950s had outgrown the space provided by the original stucco building. So, in the early 1960s Maddox enlarged the restaurant by extending the front of the building closer to Hemphill Avenue. The current building with its brick facade reflects the 1960s renovation.

Aware of the desegregation changes occurring in Atlanta and elsewhere in the late 1950s and early 1960s, Maddox, a staunch segregationist, defiantly declared that his restaurant would never be integrated. To promote his segregationist cause, Maddox took out paid advertisements in the Atlanta newspapers. Under the heading "Pickrick Says," Maddox

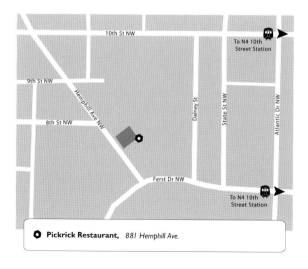

Pickrick Restaurant, *881 Hemphill Ave.*

race-baited his readers. For example, in a May 1963 "Pickrick Says" column, along with the skillet-fried chicken special of the day, Maddox reported that a caller had warned him that Martin Luther King, Jr., and Robert Kennedy were making plans to eat at the Pickrick. Maddox told the caller: "I have the key to the Pickrick and as long as I do have, the 'Great—Black Father,' the Attorney General, City Hall, the state capitol and anything or anybody else you named will not race mix The Pickrick." Then he added, "If you screwballs don't believe that, then prove me wrong."[58]

Maddox continued his resistance for several years. When prospective black customers appeared at his restaurant, he chased them away with his wooden "drumsticks" (pick handles, often incorrectly identified as ax handles), even as he employed and protected his black kitchen help and waiters. However, following President Johnson's signing of the Civil Rights Act of 1964 into law on July 2, 1964, the courts ordered Maddox to integrate his restaurant. The next day, Maddox made one defiant last stand. When three students from the Interdenominational Theological Center appeared at the restaurant, he pulled out a handgun and turned them away.

Three days later, the students filed two lawsuits— one in US District Court seeking a restraining order against Maddox for refusing to serve them as mandated in the Civil Rights Act, and the other in Fulton County Civil Court charging that Maddox had pointed his pistol at them. In the federal case, Maddox was found to be in contempt of the Civil Rights Act and was ordered to desegregate his restaurant. In response, Maddox closed the Pickrick and opened the Lester Maddox Cafeteria on the same

(top) Pickrick Restaurant in 1950s; (bottom) Former Pickrick
Restaurant in 2008

premises. However, again he was found to be in violation of the federal mandate. Finally, instead of complying with the court order, Maddox closed the restaurant in February 1965. The other case, the civil suit on the gun-pointing charge, went to trial on April 12, 1965. After only thirty-five minutes of deliberation, the all-white jury returned a not-guilty verdict.

Although Maddox lost the battle to operate a segregated restaurant, the notoriety and respect he had gained among segregationists because of his resistance catapulted him into the Georgia governor's office in the fall of 1966.

In October 1965, Maddox sold the restaurant building and property to Georgia Tech for $290,000. Georgia Tech extensively remodeled the restaurant and for many decades used the building, known as the Ajax building, as their job placement center. Currently the building is used for storage. Future plans call for the building to be demolished for green space.

"Atlanta Wall"

Peyton Rd. and Harlan Rd., SW

DIRECTIONS BY CAR FROM THE EAST Take I-20 west and exit at Hamilton E. Holmes Dr. (Exit 52A). Turn right (south) on Holmes and go 0.3 mile to the Martin Luther King, Jr. Dr. intersection. Cross over Martin Luther King, Jr. Dr. and continue one block until Holmes merges with Peyton Rd. Continue on Peyton 0.5 mile to the intersection with Harlan Rd. on the right. Two steel and wooden barricades, derisively called the "Atlanta Wall," were erected on Peyton Rd. and Harlan Rd. a short distance north of the intersection of Peyton and Harlan.

The "Atlanta Wall"

DIRECTIONS BY CAR FROM THE WEST Take I-20 east to the Hamilton E. Holmes Dr. exit (Exit 52). Turn right onto Holmes and follow the directions above.

DIRECTIONS BY MARTA Take the west line train to the Hamilton E. Holmes MARTA station (W5) and then take the No. 160 bus or walk south on Holmes following the directions above.

In December 1962, Spelman College physician, Dr. Clinton E. Warner, purchased a house in the white neighborhood of Peyton Forest in southwest Atlanta. His action precipitated a major civil rights crisis in Atlanta.

With many black families displaced from their neighborhoods by the building of Atlanta's expressways and other downtown developments in the 1950s and early 1960s, and with a rapidly growing black middle class, black demand for decent housing was very high. As blacks expanded into the southwest quadrant of the city, they soon discovered the attractiveness of Peyton Forest and Cascade Heights. However, after only preliminary inquiries, prospective black buyers learned that the whites living there strongly opposed integration. As the demand on the

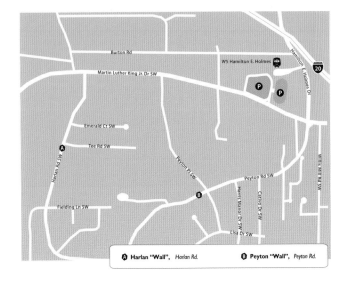

Ⓐ **Harlan "Wall"**, *Harlan Rd.*   Ⓑ **Peyton "Wall"**, *Peyton Rd.*

part of blacks increased, "blockbusting" real estate agents, both black and white, hoping to make a quick buck, moved in.

When Dr. Warner's purchase became known, some of the residents of the neighborhood panicked. "For Sale" signs sprouted up around the neighborhood. Many whites, however, did not want to leave; they simply wanted to keep their neighborhoods segregated. A group hurried to city hall and demanded that something be done to stop the movement of additional blacks into the area. Following their visit, the board of aldermen's public works committee conferred with Mayor Allen and together they devised a plan to erect a number of barricades in an effort to prevent blacks from entering the neighborhood. The board of aldermen voted approval for the plan at 5:00 P.M. on December 17. With the mayor's signature, it became a legal city ordinance.

At seven o'clock the following morning, city work crews appeared in Peyton Forest and began erecting nearly three-foot-high wood and steel barricades on

Peyton Rd. and Harlan Rd., the only two streets running north and south through the neighborhood. The two barricades were erected a short distance north of the intersection of Peyton and Harlan.

Most white residents in the neighborhood welcomed the mayor's action. Atlanta's blacks, however, reacted with intense opposition. Many demanded the immediate removal of the barricades. The Committee on Appeal for Human Rights (COAHR), co-chaired by Ralph Moore from Morehouse and Gwendolyn Iles from Spelman, along with the officers of SNCC, joined the many cries to have the barricades removed.

Journalists from across the country gave the story of Atlanta's "Berlin Wall" wide coverage. Many ridiculed Atlanta for not living up to its image as "the city too busy to hate."[59] For example, Time magazine, in an article titled "Divided City," pointed out the irony of Mayor Allen's action by quoting from his inaugural speech delivered a year earlier. In his speech the mayor had made reference to his recent visit to the Berlin Wall: "It was in Berlin that the tragic and dramatic lesson of what happens to a divided city came home to me," he said, "and if I could make you see it as I saw it, you would share with me my feeling that Atlanta must not be a city divided."[60]

On January 7, 1963, ten of the thirteen aldermen voted again to support the barricades. In response, Donald Hollowell, the attorney for those who opposed the barricades, filed a suit in Fulton County Superior Court to have the barricades removed. Hoping for an immediate court ruling, Hollowell was soon disappointed. The case was given to Judge George P. Whitman, who was in no hurry to make a decision.

Protest against the "Atlanta Wall

Finally, on March 1, 1963, Judge Whitman declared the barricades unconstitutional and ordered their immediate removal. Mayor Allen, who realized that he had made a mistake, welcomed Judge Whitman's decision. He later explained: "The day the court was supposed to render a decision I had a crew standing by at the barricade[s] waiting for the final word, and, when they were radioed the order, they completely removed all signs of them in less than twenty minutes."[61]

In his autobiography, Mayor: Notes on the Sixties, Mayor Allen admitted he had not sought sufficient advice before erecting the barricades and that he was "completely in error in trying to solve the issue in such a crude way." He said he had forgotten what former mayor William B. Hartsfield had once told him: "Never do anything wrong that they can take a picture of."[62] No evidence of the "wall" remains today.

Ruby Doris Smith Robinson Grave Site

South-View Cemetery, 1990 Jonesboro Rd. SE

www.southviewcemetery.com

DIRECTIONS BY CAR FROM THE NORTH Take 1-75-85 south to the University Ave. exit (Exit 244). Turn left onto University and go two blocks to McDonough Blvd. Turn right onto McDonough and go 0.2 mile to Jonesboro Rd. Bear right onto Jonesboro and continue 1.4 mile to the cemetery at 1990 Jonesboro Rd.

DIRECTIONS BY CAR FROM THE SOUTH Take I-75/85 north to the Langford Pkwy exit (Exit 77, GA 166). Go 0.6 mile and merge left onto Lakewood Ave. Go 1 mile and turn right onto Claire Dr. Go 0.1 mile and turn right onto Jonesboro Rd. Continue 0.4 mile to the cemetery at 1990 Jonesboro Rd.

DIRECTIONS BY BUS Take the No. 55 bus south from the Five Points MARTA station (M) to 1990 Jonesboro Rd., SE.

Ruby Doris Smith (Robinson) was born on April 25, 1942, at 794 Fraser Street in Summerhill, a black neighborhood in southwest Atlanta (a few blocks from where Turner Field, the Atlanta Braves' stadium, now stands). She attended elementary school in Summerhill and graduated from Price High School in spring 1958. In fall 1958 she entered

SACRED PLACES   FOUR SCATTERED SITES

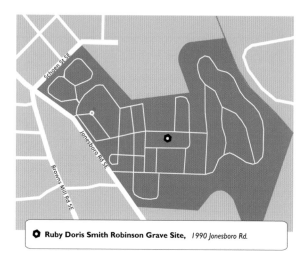

● **Ruby Doris Smith Robinson Grave Site,** *1990 Jonesboro Rd.*

Spelman College and graduated seven years later. It took her seven years to complete the usual four years of work because she had dropped out several times to participate in the movement—participation that included several lengthy stays in jail. Her most lengthy incarcerations were thirty-one days in the York County Jail in Rock Hill, South Carolina; three weeks in the Hinds County Jail in Jackson, Mississippi; and three weeks in Mississippi's Parchman Penitentiary.

Two months after graduation, in July 1965, Ruby Doris gave birth to a son, Kenneth Toure (named after President Sékou Touré whom she had met in Guinea). In May 1966, she was elected executive secretary of SNCC, replacing Jim Forman, who had resigned after serving for several years. At the same time, Stokely Carmichael was elected chair and Cleveland

Mug Shot of Ruby Doris Smith taken in Hinds County Jail in Jackson, Mississippi on June 2, 1961.

Sellers was elected program secretary. Ruby Doris was the only woman ever elected executive secretary of SNCC, a position she held until shortly before her death in October 1967.

Ruby Doris Smith Robinson (1966)

In January 1967, while in New York City to attend a SNCC fundraising event, Ruby Doris became ill and was admitted to Beth Israel Hospital. After many tests, she was diagnosed with terminal cancer. In June, she was transferred from New York to Grady Hospital in Atlanta. The doctors at Grady realized that there was little they could do for her, so they discharged her into the care of her family. She died at home on October 27, 1967. She was twenty-five years old. Survivors included her husband, Clifford; their two-year-old son, Kenneth Toure; her parents; four brothers; and two sisters.

Ruby Doris's husband, Clifford, recalled that at some point in their marriage Ruby Doris told him she wanted to work in the movement for the rest of her life. Of course, that is exactly what she did.

Funeral services for Ruby Doris were held on Saturday, October 14, at the West Mitchell Christian Methodist Episcopal (CME) Church, the church with which she had been affiliated since her birth. She was buried in South-View Cemetery (chartered April 21, 1886) in south Atlanta. On her grave the family placed a simple ground-level marker with her name and the dates of her birth (April 24, 1942) and death (October 7, 1967). Thirty-one years later, in 1998, her family replaced the simple marker with a granite headstone. On the headstone, in addition to

Ruby Doris's name and the dates of her birth and death, the family added Ruby Doris's motto as an epitaph: "If You Think Free, You Are Free."

Ruby Doris Smith Robinson's Obituary

We are tired of writing obituaries for the wrong people, tired of repeating how fine and strong and beautiful are the movement people who die. They die and are killed and eaten away by the pain of struggling against a killer society. More will die, we know, and may the strength of all of them seep into those of us left living. The oppressors die at an old age and the liberators young. May we see the day when this is reversed.... The young years that Ruby Doris Robinson put into SNCC were not wasted. They have helped many thousands live and struggle.[63]

Other Atlanta notables discussed in this guide who are buried in South-View Cemetery include

Alonzo Herndon (1858–1927) and his two wives, **Adrienne (McNeil) Herndon** (1869–1910) and **Jessie (Gillespie) Herndon** (1871–1947); **John Wesley Dobbs** (1882–1961) and his wife, **Irene (Thompson) Dobbs** (1885–1972); **Martin Luther King, Sr.** (1899–1984) and his wife, **Alberta (Williams) King** (1904–1974); **Horace Mann Bond** (1904–1972) and his wife, **Julia (Washington) Bond** (1908–2007); and **William Holmes Borders** (1905–1993) and his wife, **Julia (Pate) Borders** (1907–1965).

The locations of these gravesites as well as information about the individuals can be obtained at the cemetery office.

Epilogue

During the time Sacred Places was in production, a new civil rights memorial was unveiled in downtown Atlanta. The memorial, dedicated to Andrew Young, was unveiled in Walton Spring Park on April 14, 2008.

Andrew Young Memorial

On island at intersection of Spring St., Andrew Young International Blvd., and Carnegie Way, NW

DIRECTIONS BY CAR FROM THE NORTH Take I-75/85 south to Williams St. (Exit 249C). Go 0.5 mile to Andrew Young International Blvd. Turn left and go one block to the Andrew Young Memorial.

DIRECTIONS BY CAR FROM THE SOUTH Take I-75/85 north Andrew Young International Blvd. (Exit 248C). Turn left onto Andrew Young International Blvd. and continue 0.7 mile to the Andrew Young Memorial.

DIRECTIONS BY MARTA Take the north line train to the Peachtree Center station (N1). Exit the station on the Peachtree St. side. Turn left and walk 1/2 block to Andrew Young International Blvd., then turn right and continue one block to the Andrew Young Memorial.

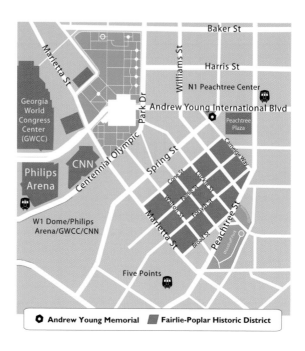

Map legend:
⬡ Andrew Young Memorial ▮ Fairlie-Poplar Historic District

Bankrolled by Atlanta businessman Charles Loudermilk, the memorial features two artistic creations: 1) a circular plaza with a twenty-five-foot obelisk cascading water down its four sides and standing on a mosaic floor of bronze tiles inscribed with references to Young's many services to the city, country, and the world. Surrounding the obelisk is a semi-circular granite bench and a wall containing five glass panels engraved with quotations by Young; 2) an 8.5-foot bronze statue of Young standing with outstretched arms.

The park was designed by landscape architect Leo Alvarez, the obelisk was created by Atlanta sculptor Curtis Patterson, and the statue is the work of North Carolina sculptor John Paul Harris. Patterson said his contribution to the memorial is meant to be a reflective space.

Andrew Young Memorial

Echoing Patterson, Atlanta mayor Shirley Franklin declared that the park provides a serene place that will "allow us to come, meditate and think about world peace, friendships, social justice and the many contributions of Andrew Young."[64]

Young was active in the civil rights movement from the late 1950s to the early 1970s. However, his most formal years with the movement were from 1961 to 1968 when, as a member and, for many years, executive secretary of the Southern Christian Leadership Conference, he worked closely with Martin Luther King, Jr., and others in the SCLC to organize civil rights campaigns and marches in Albany, Georgia (1961–1962); Birmingham, Alabama (1963); the March on Washington (1963); St. Augustine, Florida (1964); Mississippi Freedom Summer (1964); and the Selma-to-Montgomery

March (1965). When King was assassinated on the balcony of the Lorraine Hotel in Memphis on April 4, 1968, Young was by his side.

In 1972, Young was elected to Congress from the Fifth District of Georgia, a position he held until 1977 when President Jimmy Carter appointed him US Ambassador to the United Nations. Young resigned from the UN in 1979 and subsequently served two terms as mayor of Atlanta (1981–1989). In the early and mid-1990s, Young co-chaired (with businessman Billy Payne) the Atlanta Committee for the 1996 Olympic Games.

Not far from the memorial is the office of GoodWorks International (303 Peachtree St. NE), the organization Young founded and heads that focuses on providing economic opportunities between the US and African and Caribbean countries.

Chronology of Civil Rights Events in Atlanta

(or of Importance to Atlanta, 1957–1968)

1957

JANUARY The NAACP holds a rally at the Big Bethel AME Church on Auburn Avenue to discuss the ending of segregation in Atlanta on January 1.

A group of black Atlanta ministers organize the Triple L Movement (Law, Love, and Liberation) to challenge the segregated seated patterns on Atlanta's buses and trolleys.

Students in Spelman College's Social Science Club, along with their adviser, Howard Zinn, sit together in the "white" section of the balcony at the Georgia Legislature and are forced to move.

1958

JANUARY Students in Spelman College's Social Science Club, along with their adviser, Howard Zinn, sit together in the "white" section of the balcony of the Georgia Legislature and, as happened a year earlier, are forced to move.

OCTOBER 12 White supremacists bomb The Temple on Peachtree Street in response to Rabbi Jacob Rothchild's support of the civil rights movement.

1959

MAY Atlanta University Center (AUC) students and faculty are involved in the desegregation of the Atlanta Public Library. On May 22, Dr. Irene Dobbs Jackson, professor of French at Spelman, is the first African American to receive a library card.

JULY The first Southwide Institute on Nonviolent Resistance to Segregation is organized at Spelman College with sixty-five individuals in attendance.

1960

FEBRUARY 1 Martin Luther King, Jr., and family move from Montgomery, Alabama, to Atlanta. King becomes co-pastor with his father at Ebenezer Baptist Church and works as president of the Southern Christian Leadership Conference in the SCLC office on Auburn Avenue.

FEBRUARY 1 Four African-American male students from North Carolina A & T College sit down at a "white" lunch counter in Woolworth's department store in Greensboro, North Carolina.

FEBRUARY 3 Inspired by the sit-ins in Greensboro, two Morehouse College students, Lonnie King and Julian Bond, invite AUC students to a meeting in Sale Hall on the campus of Morehouse to discuss plans for possible demonstrations in Atlanta. Approximately twelve students attend.

MARCH 9 The statement, "An Appeal for Human Rights," is published in the *Atlanta Constitution,* the *Atlanta Journal,* and the *Atlanta Daily World.* The statement, written by a group of students from the Atlanta University Center (AUC), is signed by a representative from each of the six schools in the AUC.

MARCH 10 A group of AUC students and faculty desegregate the Atlanta Municipal Auditorium as they attend a performance of *My Fair Lady.*

MARCH 10 AUC students found the organization Committee On Appeal For Human Rights (COAHR) to coordinate their civil rights activities.

MARCH 15 AUC students organize their first sit-in at ten lunch counters in Atlanta. Two hundred students participate. Seventy-seven are arrested.

APRIL 10 Martin Luther King, Jr., delivers the Founders' Day speech at Spelman College. In his speech, "Keep Moving from This Mountain," he lauds the students for their participation in the civil rights movement.

APRIL 15–17 The organizing conference of the Student Nonviolent Coordinating Committee (SNCC) is held at Shaw University in Raleigh, North Carolina. Several AUC students attend.

APRIL 16–21 AUC students picket the A & P supermarkets at 242 Edgewood Avenue and 337 Boulevard Avenue in order to pressure the stores to increase their black employment.

APRIL Spelman College student, Marian Wright, speaks about civil rights at Agnes Scott College in Decatur, Georgia.

MAY 13–14 First official meeting of the Temporary Student Nonviolent Coordinating Committee is held on the campus of Atlanta University.

MAY 17 On the sixth anniversary of the *Brown v. Board of Education* Supreme Court decision, close to 3000 AUC students march to the state capitol. When the police prevent the students from approaching the capitol, they divert the march to the Wheat Street Baptist Church, where they hold a rally. In the evening, the AUC students organize an entertaining fundraising event known as "Sit-In Showdown" in Davage Auditorium at Clark College.

JUNE AND JULY   AUC students and supporters organize a boycott of Rich's department store.

JULY 31   AUC students begin publication of the *Atlanta Inquirer* to provide coverage of their civil rights activities the other Atlanta newspapers failed to cover.

AUGUST 6   *The Nation* publishes Howard Zinn's article, "A Finishing School for Pickets," about Spelman College students' civil rights activities.

AUGUST 7 AND 14   AUC students participate in "kneel-ins" at several Atlanta churches.

OCTOBER 19   AUC students organize sit-ins at eight downtown lunch counters. Lonnie King from Morehouse College and Herschelle Sullivan from Spelman College invite Martin Luther King, Jr., to join the students at Rich's. King and fifty-one students are arrested.

OCTOBER 26   Following his arrest at Rich's, Martin Luther King, Jr., is convicted of violating his probation on an earlier minor driving conviction and is sentenced to four months of hard labor at Reidsville State Prison. He is released after one day. His arrest and conviction become an issue in the 1960 presidential election and influence a substantial number of blacks to vote for John Kennedy. This support helps him win the election over Richard Nixon.

NOVEMBER 25–26   As AUC students picket downtown stores, a group of Ku Klux Klansmen parade across the street.

1961

FEBRUARY 7 Spelman College student Ruby Doris Smith and others are arrested for sitting-in at segregated lunch counters in Rock Hill, South Carolina, and serve thirty-one days in the York County Jail.

MID-FEBRUARY Many AUC students are arrested during sit-ins at downtown lunch counters and serve ten days in the Fulton County Jail.

MARCH 6 COAHR, the chamber of commerce, and Atlanta businessmen reach an agreement on a plan to desegregate public lunch counters and rest rooms in the fall of 1961. (The agreement was only partially carried out.)

MARCH 10 An emotional meeting to discuss the March 6 desegregation plan is held at the Warren Memorial United Methodist Church, 131 Ashby Street. Martin Luther King, Sr., is booed by the audience. Martin Luther King, Jr., quiets the rowdy crowd with a conciliatory speech.

MAY 4 Thirteen Freedom Riders (7 blacks and 6 whites) board two buses in Washington, DC, with the purpose of testing the South's compliance with the 1960 Supreme Court decision *(Boyton v. Virginia)* on the desegregation of interstate bus terminals. Included among the seven blacks was Charles Person, a Morehouse College freshman.

MAY 17 Herschelle Sullivan from Spelman College, Lonnie King and Charles Lyles from Morehouse College, and Benjamin Brown from Clark College file a federal lawsuit against discrimination in all city-owned facilities such as parks, swimming pools, tennis courts, the municipal auditorium, and the municipal courts. Fifteen months later, on August 27, 1962, the federal court rules in the students' favor.

MAY 19 Spelman College student Ruby Doris Smith joins the Freedom Riders in Birmingham, travels with them to Montgomery where a number of the riders (not including Ruby Doris) are injured, and then travels to Jackson, Mississippi, where she is arrested. Following three weeks in the Hinds County Jail in Jackson, Ruby Doris and others are transferred to Parchman Penitentiary where they remain for three more weeks.

AUGUST As mandated by the federal court, several Atlanta public high schools begin the process of desegregation by admitting nine black students.

NOVEMBER AND DECEMBER Protests and sit-ins are organized in Albany, Georgia. Many students from Albany State College participate in the demonstrations and are arrested. William Dennis, Jr., Albany State president, expels forty students because of their participation in the protests. Three of the expelled students, Janie Culbreth, Annette Jones, and Bernice Johnson, transfer to Spelman College in January 1962.

DECEMBER 10 Lenora Taitt, who graduated from Spelman College in the spring of 1961, joins seven others on a train for a Freedom Ride from Atlanta to Albany to test compliance with the November 1 desegregation ruling of the Interstate Commerce Commission (ICC). Upon their arrival in Albany, all eight are arrested and Lenora spends ten days in the Dougherty County Jail in Albany.

1962

FEBRUARY 15–17 AUC students travel to Washington, DC, to participate in a peace demonstration with six thousand other students from across the country.

JUNE Spelman College student Ruby Doris Smith and seven other plaintiffs file a federal lawsuit against Grady Hospital, charging that the hospital practiced racial discrimination and segregation. The suit failed.

JULY   The National Association for the Advancement of Colored People (NAACP) holds its fifty-third annual convention in Atlanta's Municipal Auditorium.

FALL 1962 THROUGH SPRING 1963   AUC students participate in demonstrations against two barricades erected on December 18, 1962, on Peyton and Harlan Roads in southwest Atlanta at the direction of Mayor Ivan Allen, Jr., and the board of aldermen. The nearly three-foot-high wood and steel barricades, which became known as the "Atlanta Wall," were an attempt to prevent blacks from purchasing houses in Peyton Forest and Cascade Heights. The barricades remained until March 1, 1963, when they were ordered removed by a superior court judge.

1963

FEBRUARY   With the participation of nearly five hundred civic organizations and local ministers, Operation Breadbasket launches a selective-buying campaign against Highland Bakeries after the company refused to provide new jobs for blacks or promote current black employees.

MARCH 13   Five AUC students participate in a "lie-in" at Henry Grady Hotel in downtown Atlanta. Two of the five are arrested.

MARCH 14   Several hundred AUC students march from the Henry Grady Hotel to City Hall to demand that Mayor Allen "take action immediately regarding the breaking down of racial barriers." On the steps of city hall, Spelman College student Gwendolyn Iles reads a letter of concern to the mayor.

MAY 3   Two thousand young demonstrators are assaulted by dogs and police officers wielding high-pressure fire hoses in Kelly Ingram Park in Birmingham, Alabama.

JUNE Howard Zinn, professor of history and chair of the social science department at Spelman College, is fired for encouraging students to participate in civil rights demonstrations and to demand more student freedoms.

AUGUST 28 AUC students participate in the March on Washington.

DECEMBER 8 Spelman College's YMCA organizes a symposium on the pending civil rights bill.

DECEMBER More than three thousand adults and students march on a "Pilgrimage for Democracy" from Herndon Stadium at Morris Brown College to Hurt Park downtown. Martin Luther King, Jr., is the main speaker at a rally held in Hurt Park.

1964

JANUARY AUC students organize a series of sit-ins at downtown lunch counters. Among the many students arrested is Spelman student Mardon Walker, a white exchange student from Connecticut College for Women. On February 19 she is convicted of violating Georgia's anti-trespass law and is sentenced to six months in jail, twelve months on the public works, and a $1,000 fine. She appealed her case to the Georgia Supreme Court, which upheld her conviction. She then appealed to the US Supreme Court, which, on May 24, 1965, overturned her conviction.

JANUARY 27 Spelman College instructor Gloria Bishop (later Gloria Wade-Gayles) is arrested in a demonstration at Leb's Restaurant downtown and spends nearly five days in an Atlanta jail. Her article about her experience, "Four and Half Days in Atlanta's Jails," is published in the July 1964 issue of the *Atlantic Monthly.*

SPRING A number of AUC students, including Gwendolyn Robinson from Spelman, are arrested at the Pickrick, a restaurant owned by Lester Maddox, and spend a night in jail. A short time later, Gwen and other Spelman students are arrested at a Krystal restaurant and spend three nights in jail. After Robinson's second arrest and incarceration, Spelman's dean of students instructs Gwen to pack her bags and leave Spelman. A large number of AUC students protest Gwen's expulsion and she is put under strict probation and allowed to finished the spring semester.

SUMMER A large number of AUC students participate in the Mississippi Freedom Summer. Former Spelman College instructor Staughton Lynd serves as the director of the Freedom Schools.

JULY 2 President Johnson signs the Civil Rights Act of 1964.

SEPTEMBER 11–OCTOBER 4 Eleven SNCC staff members, including Morehouse student Julian Bond and Spelman College student Ruby Doris Smith Robinson, visit the west African country of Guinea as the guests of President Sékou Touré.

NOVEMBER At the SNCC staff retreat in Waveland, Mississippi, Mary King and Casey Hayden submit a controversial paper about sexism in SNCC.

DECEMBER 10 Martin Luther King, Jr., receives the Nobel Peace Prize in Oslo, Norway.

1965

JANUARY 27 Martin Luther King, Jr., is honored for receiving the Nobel Peace Prize at an integrated dinner attended by 1500 at the Dinkler Hotel in downtown Atlanta.

MARCH 7 "Bloody Sunday," an attack on marchers at the Edmund Pettus Bridge in Selma, Alabama, occurs.

MARCH 21–25 Several hundred march from Selma to Montgomery.

AUGUST 6 President Johnson signs the Voting Rights Act of 1965.

1966

JANUARY SNCC organizes the "Atlanta Project," a community organizing effort in the Atlanta neighborhood of Vine City.

MAY Former Spelman College student Ruby Doris Smith Robinson is elected executive secretary of SNCC. She is the only woman ever elected to that position. At the same time, in a very controversial election, Stokely Carmichael replaces John Lewis as chair of SNCC.

SEPTEMBER 22, 28, AND OCTOBER 6 Spelman College president Albert E. Manley delivers a three-part lecture series on "The Negro Rebellion—Past, Present, and Future" in Spelman's Sisters Chapel.

1967

JANUARY Former Spelman College student Ruby Doris Smith Robinson becomes ill while fund raising for SNCC in New York City and is admitted to Beth Israel Hospital. After a series of tests she is diagnosed with terminal cancer.

JUNE Ruby Doris is transferred from New York to Grady Hospital in Atlanta and after a short stay is sent home to be cared for by her family.

OCTOBER 7 Ruby Doris dies at home at the age of twenty-five. She is survived by her parents; her husband, Clifford; her two-year old son, Kenneth Toure; four brothers; and two sisters.

OCTOBER 14 Ruby Doris's funeral is held at West Mitchell CME Church. Following the funeral she is buried in South-View Cemetery in south Atlanta. A simple flat stone inscribed with her name and birth and death dates (April 24, 1942 and October 7, 1967) is placed on her grave. (In 1998, Ruby Doris's family replaced the simple flat stone with an upright headstone carved with the following epitaph: "If You Think Free, You are Free.")

1968

APRIL 4 March Luther King, Jr., is killed in Memphis, Tennessee.

APRIL 7–8 Eighty thousand mourners view Martin Luther King, Jr.'s body as he lay in state in Sisters Chapel at Spelman College.

APRIL 9 The funeral for Martin Luther King, Jr., is held at Ebenezer Baptist Church. Following the service his body is carried on a mule-drawn wagon to his alma mater, Morehouse College. Two hundred thousand mourners follow the caisson, and 50,000 crowd on to the quadrangle shared by Morehouse and Atlanta University to honor Dr. King. Benjamin E. Mays, president of Morehouse, eulogizes his former student from the steps of Harkness Hall. King is buried in a crypt in South-View Cemetery. (In 1970 the crypt was moved to the King Center on Auburn Avenue.)

Bibliography

Atlanta Regional Council for Higher Education, "Atlanta in the Civil Rights Movement." www.atlantahighered.org/civilrights.

Allen, Ivan, Jr. *Mayor: Notes on the Sixties*. New York: Simon and Schuster, 1971.

Atlanta Committee for Cooperative Action. *Atlanta: A Second Look*. Atlanta: Allied Printing, 1960.

Bishop, Gloria Wade. "Four and a Half Days in Atlanta's Jails." *Atlantic Monthly* 214/1 (July 1964): 68–70.

Blackburn-Beamon, Juliet. "The Library Card." *Spelman Messenger* 98/4 (1982/83): 41.

Bond, Julian. "The Politics of Civil Rights History." In *New Directions in Civil Rights Studies*. Edited by Armstead L. Robinson and Patricia Sullivan. Charlottesville: University Press of Virginia, 1991. 8–16.

————. "The Students Won the Victory and the Adults Negotiated the Truce." In *Refuse to Stand Silently By: An Oral History of Grass Roots Social Activism in America, 1921–1964*. Edited and with an introduction by Eliot Wigginton. New York: Doubleday, 1991. 315–33.

Challenor, Herschelle. "Untold Stories and Unsung Heroes." *Clark Atlanta Magazine* (Spring 2001): 12–17.

Cobb, Charles E., Jr. *On the Road to Freedom: A Guided Tour of the Civil Rights Trail*. Chapel Hill: Algonquin, 2008. 159–78.

Davis, Townsend. *Weary Feet, Rested Souls: A Guided History of the Civil Rights Movement*. New York: W. W. Norton, 1998. 139–62.

Drimmer, Melvin. "The Future of Spelman and the Atlanta University Center in an Age of Blackness." *Spelman Messenger* 85/3 (May 1969): 22–25, 28–30.

Edelman, Marian Wright. *Lanterns: A Memoir of Mentors*. Boston: Beacon Press, 1999.

English, James W. *The Prophet of Wheat Street: The Story of William Holmes Borders, a Man Who Refused to Fail*. Elgin IL: David C. Cook Publishing Co., 1973.

Fleming, Cynthia. *Soon We Will Not Cry: The Liberation of Ruby Doris Smith Robinson*. Lanham MD: Rowman & Littlefield, 1998.

———. "Black Women and Black Power: The Case of Ruby Doris Smith Robinson and the Student Nonviolent Coordinating Committee." In *Sisters in the Struggle: African-American Women in the Civil Rights-Black Power Movement*. Edited by Betty Collier-Thomas and V. P. Franklin. New York: New York University Press, 2001. 197–213.

Forman, James. *The Making of Black Revolutionaries.* Washington DC: Open Hand Publishing, 1985.

Fort, Vincent. "The Atlanta Sit-In Movement, 1960–1961, An Oral Study." In *Atlanta, Georgia, 1960–1961: Sit-Ins and Student Activism*. Edited by David J. Garrow. Brooklyn NY: Carlson, 1989. 113–80.

Garrow, David J., editor. *Atlanta, Georgia, 1960–61: Sit-Ins and Student Activism*. Brooklyn NY: Carlson, 1989.

Grady-Willis, Winston A. *Challenging U.S. Apartheid: Atlanta and Black Struggles for Human Rights, 1960–1977*. Durham: Duke University Press, 2006.

Hampton, Henry and Steve Fayer. *Voices of Freedom: An Oral History of the Civil Rights Movement from the 1950s through the 1980s*. New York: Bantam Books, 1990.

Harmon, David. *Beneath the Image of the Civil Rights Movement and Race Relations: Atlanta, Georgia, 1946–1981*. New York: Garland, 1996.

Harris, Jessica. "An Interview with Alice Walker." *Essence* 7/3 (July 1976): 33.

Hollowell, Louise and Martin C. Lehfeldt. *The Sacred Call: A Tribute to Donald Hollowell, Civil Rights Champion*. Winter Park FL: FOUR-G Publishers, Inc., 1997.

Hunter-Gault, Charlayne. "For Ruby Doris, Hopefully." *Spelman Messenger* 97/3 (Celebration Issue 1981): 19.

King, Martin Luther, Jr. "Keep Moving from This Mountain." *Spelman Messenger* 76/3 (May 1960): 6–17.

King, Mary. *Freedom Song: A Personal Story of the 1960s Civil Rights Movement*. New York: William Morrow, 1987.

Lefever, Harry G. *Undaunted By The Fight: Spelman College and the Civil Rights Movement, 1957–1967*. Macon GA: Mercer University Press, 2005.

Lewis, John. *Walking with the Wind: A Memoir of the Movement*. New York: Simon & Schuster, 1998.

Lincoln, C. Eric. "The Strategy of a Sit-in." In *Atlanta, Georgia, 1960–61: Sit-Ins and Student Activism*. Edited by David J. Garrow. Brooklyn NY: Carlson, 1961. 95–103.

Long, Margaret. "Let Freedom Sing." *The Progressive* 29 (November 1965): 27–31.

Manley, Albert E. *A Legacy Continues: The Manley Years at Spelman College, 1953–1976*. Lanham MD: University Press of America, 1995.

———. "The Negro Rebellion—Past, Present, and Future." Mimeographed document in Emory University Library's general collection, 1966.

Mason, Herman "Skip," Jr. *Politics, Civil Rights, and Law in Black Atlanta 1870–1970*. Charleston SC: Arcadia, 2000.

Mays, Benjamin E. *Born to Rebel*. Athens: University of Georgia Press, 1987.

Neary, John. *Julian Bond: Black Rebel*. New York: William Morrow, 1971.

Newsom, Lionel and William Gorden. "A Stormy Rally in Atlanta." In *Atlanta, Georgia, 1960–1961: Sit-Ins and Student Activism*. Edited by David J. Garrow. Brooklyn NY: Carlson, 1989. 105–12.

Nystrom, Justin. "Segregation's Last Stand: Lester Maddox and the Transformation of Atlanta." *Atlanta History*, xlv/2 (Summer 2001): 35–51.

Olson, Lynn. *Freedom's Daughters: The Unsung Heroines of the Civil Rights Movement from 1830 to 1970*. New York: Scribner, 2001.

Pomerantz, Gary M. *Where Peachtree Meets Sweet Auburn: The Saga of Two Families and the Making of Atlanta*. New York: Scribner, 1996.

Raines, Howard. *My Soul Is Rested: The Story of the Civil Rights Movement in the Deep South*. New York: Penguin Books, 1983.

Reagon, Bernice Johnson. "Voices of the Civil Rights Movement: Black American Freedom Songs 1960–1966." Washington DC: Smithsonian Folkways Recordings, 1997. 2 compact discs.

———. Interview with Marvette Pérez. *Radical History Review* 68 (Spring 1997): 4–24.

————. "Bernice Johnson Reagon: The Singing Warrior." Videotape and transcript of interview with Rachel E. Harding and Vincent G. Harding, October 27, 1997. Denver CO: The Veterans of Hope Project, Iliff School of Theology, 2000.

Royster, Jacqueline Jones. "A 'Heartbeat' For Liberation: The Reclamation of Ruby Doris Smith." *Sage: A Scholarly Journal on Black Women* 4 (student supplement 1988): 64–66.

Simmons, Gwendolyn Zoharah [Gwendolyn Robinson]. "Gwendolyn Zoharah Simmons: Following the Call." Videotape and transcript of interview with Vincent G. Harding and Sudarshan Kapur, June 24 and 25, 1998. Denver CO: The Veterans of Hope Project, Iliff School of Theology, 2000.

————. "Striving for Muslim Women's Human Rights—Before and Beyond Beijing: An African American Perspective." In *Windows of Faith: Muslim Women Scholar-Activists in North America*. Edited by Gisela Webb. Syracuse NY: Syracuse University Press, 2000. 197–225.

Southern Regional Council. "Will the Circle be Unbroken," 1997. www.southerncouncil.org (Radio series).

The Student Voice, 1960–1965: Periodical of the Student Nonviolent Coordinating Committee. Compiled by the staff of the Martin Luther King, Jr., Papers Project. Clayborne Carson, senior editor and director. Westport CT: Meckler, 1990.

University Microfilms, Inc. "The Student Nonviolent Coordinating Committee Papers, 1959–1972: A Guide to the Microfilm Edition," Ann Arbor MI, 1994.

Vanlandingham, Karen. "In Pursuit of a Changing Dream: Spelman College Students and the Civil Rights Movement, 1955–1962." Masters thesis, Emory University, 1985.

Wade-Gayles, Gloria. *Pushed Back to Strength: A Black Woman's Journey Home*. New York: Avon Books, 1993.

Walker, Alice. *Meridian.* New York: Simon & Schuster, 1976.

————. *In Search of Our Mothers' Gardens.* New York: Harcourt, Brace Jovanovich, 1983.

Walker, Jack. "Sit-Ins in Atlanta: A Study in the Negro Revolt." In *Atlanta, Georgia, 1960–1961: Sit-Ins and Student Activism*. Edited by David J. Garrow. Brooklyn NY: Carlson, 1989. 59–93.

Watters, Pat. *Down to Now: Reflections on the Southern Civil Rights Movement.* Athens: University of Georgia Press, 1993.

Zinn, Howard. "A Case of Quiet Social Change." *The Crisis* 66/8 (October 1959): 471–76.

———. *Disobedience and Democracy*. New York: Vintage, 1968.

———. "A Finishing School for Pickets." *The Nation* 119/4 (August 6, 1960): 71–73.

———. *The Southern Mystique*. New York: Alfred A. Knopf, 1964.

———. *SNCC: The New Abolitionists*. Boston: Beacon Press, 1965.

———. *You Can't Be Neutral on a Moving Train: A Personal History of Our Times*. Boston: Beacon Press, 1994.

Notes

1 Macon GA: Mercer University Press, 2005.

2 Bruce Galphin, "Negroes to Renew Bus Integration Push Here Today," *Atlanta Constitution*, January 10, 1957, 1.

3 Howard Zinn, *The Southern Mystique* (New York: Alfred A. Knopf, 1964) 116.

4 Ibid., 116–17.

5 Juliet Blackurn-Beamon, "The Library Card," *Spelman Messenger* 98/4 (1982/83): 41.

6 "Vandiver's Statement on Student Ad," *Atlanta Constitution*, March 10, 1960, 15.

7 Ibid., 1, 14.

8 Martin Luther King, Jr., "Keep Moving from This Mountain," *Spelman Messenger* 76/3 (May 1960): 13.

9 *Atlanta Inquirer,* July 31, 1960, 4.

10 "The Student Movement and You," flyer, July 1960.

11 Letter of John Wesley Dobbs to Rich's Inc., September 16, 1960, in Richard H. Rich Papers, Box 37, Folder 2, Special Collections, Robert W. Woodruff Library, Emory University, Atlanta GA.

12 Howard Raines, *My Soul Is Rested: The Story of the Civil Rights Movement in the Deep South* (New York: Penguin Books, 1983) 90.

13 Evan Thomas, *Robert Kennedy: His Life* (New York: Simon & Schuster, 2000) 102.

14 A copy of the lawsuit is in the Atlanta Student Movement box in the Woodruff Library Archives, Atlanta University Center.

15 "Court, Not Street, Is Proper Setting," *Atlanta Constitution*, May 18, 1961, 4.

16 "Plaintiffs Hail Decision," *Atlanta Inquirer*, September 1, 1962, 16.

17 Zinn, *Southern Mystique,* 138.

18 The seven other plaintiffs were Dr. Roy C. Bell, Dr. Clinton Warner, Alice Banks Smith (Ruby Doris's mother), Edwin Smith, the Reverend J. A. Middleton, Dorothy Cotton, and Septima Clark. At the time, Warner was Spelman physician, and Bell, Middleton,

Cotton, and Clark were all active with the Southern Christian Leadership Conference (SCLC).

19 "Atlanta Students Demand Death of All Jim Crow," *Jet* 23/23 (March 28, 1963): 9.

20 A copy of Gwendolyn's letter is in co-author Lefever's possession.

21 Stanley S. Scott, "Mayor Lauds Students for Orderly Protest," *Atlanta Constitution*, March 15, 1963, 3.

22 Mardon's letter is in the Nan Pendergrast Papers, Special Collections, Robert W. Woodruff Library, Emory University, Atlanta GA.

23 Gwendolyn Zoharah Simmons, "Little Memphis Girl Comes of Age in the Freedom Struggle of the 60s," unpublished manuscript in the possession of co-author Lefever, n.d., 14.

24 Margaret Long, "Let Freedom Sing," *The Progressive* (November 1965) 30-31.

25 Gloria Bishop is now Gloria Wade-Gayles. She holds the Eminent Scholar's Chair in Scholarship and Service at Spelman.

26 Gloria Wade-Gayles, *Pushed Back To Strength: A Black Woman's Journey Home* (New York: Avon, 1993) 143.

27 Gloria Wade Bishop, "Four and a Half Days in Atlanta's Jails," *Atlantic Monthly* 214/1 (July 1964): 68–70.

28 James M. Washington, *A Testament of Hope: The Essential Writings of Martin Luther King, Jr.* (San Francisco: Harper & Row, 1986) 224.

29 "Splendid victory for 'the concerned,'" *Life* (February 12, 1965): 4.

30 Ivan Allen, *Mayor: Notes on the Sixties* (New York: Simon and Schuster, 1971) 97.

31 All MARTA stations are identified by letter or by letter and number. The Five Points Station is the mid-point (M). Each of the stations on the east, west, north, and south lines is identified by letter and number (E1, E2, etc.).

32 The official death count of the riot was ten blacks and two whites. However, recent research has documented that at least fifty blacks and six whites died and hundreds, mostly blacks, were injured. On the most recent findings, see David Fort Godshalk, *Veiled Visions: The 1906 Atlanta Race Riot and the Reshaping of American Race Relations* (Chapel Hill: University of North Carolina Press, 2005) 105–106.

33 Dobbs's grandson, Maynard Jackson, became Atlanta's first black mayor in 1974. He served three terms: 1974–1978, 1978–1982, and 1990–1994.

34 Martin Luther King, Jr., *Stride Toward Freedom: The Montgomery Story* (New York: Harper & Row, 1958) 85.

35 Clayborne Carson and Peter Holloran, eds., *A Knock at Midnight: Inspiration from the Great Sermons of Reverend Martin Luther King, Jr.* (New York: Warner Books, 1998) 185–86.

36 SCLC/W.O.M.E.N., Inc., http://www.sclcwomeninc.org.

37 SCLC/W.O.M.E.N., Inc., "Civil Rights Heritage Educational Tour," http://www.sclcwomeninc.org/heritage_tour.html.

38 For more details on the drama, see Gregory D. Coleman, *We're Heaven Bound! Portrait of a Black Sacred Drama* (Athens: University of Georgia Press, 1994).

39 APEX Museum, http://www.apexmuseum.org/HOME.html.

40 Ibid.

41 APEX Museum, "Africa: the Untold Story," http://www.apex-museum.org/EXHIBITS.html.

42 "About Us: Who We Are and What We Are," Auburn Avenue Research Library, http://www.af.public.lib.ga.us/aarl.

43 Howard Thurman, *Jesus and the Disinherited* (New York: Abingdon-Cokesbury, 1949).

44 Ibid., 34.

45 Lionel Newsom and William Gorden, "A Stormy Rally in Atlanta," in *Atlanta, Georgia, 1960-1961: Sit-ins and Student Activism*. Edited by David J. Garrow (Brooklyn NY: Carlson, 1989) 108.

46 Southern Regional Council, "The Atlanta Student Movement," episode 22 of the radio series *Will the Circle Be Unbroken?*, 1997, transcript pages 16-17. Information about the series is available from the Southern Regional Council (www.southerncouncil.org). Also, the Emory University Special Collections section of the Robert W. Woodruff Library has audiotapes and transcripts, as well as other supporting materials related to the series (http://marbl.library.emory.edu). Search for "Will the Circle Be Unbroken?"

47 Gwendolyn Zoharah Simmons, "Gwendolyn Zoharah Simmons: Following the Call," videotape and transcript of interview by Vincent G. Harding and Sudarshan Kapur, June 24 and 25, 1998 (Denver CO: The Veterans of Hope Project, Iliff School of Theology 2000) 14.

48 "Herndon Home," www.nps.gov/nr/travel/atlanta/her.htm.

49 Mary King, *Freedom Song: A Personal Story of the 1960s Civil Rights Movement* (New York: William Morrow, 1987) 35.

50 Ibid., 164.

51 Jim Tharpe, "Last day's meals at Paschal's bittersweet," *Atlanta Journal Constitution*, July 29, 2003, B1.

52 Ernie Suggs, "Paschal's Passing," *Atlanta Journal Constitution*, July 27, 2003, C1.

53 Ibid., C10.

54 John Lewis, *Walking with the Wind: A Memoir of the Movement* (New York: Simon & Schuster, 1998) 320.

55 *The Autobiography of Martin Luther King, Jr.* Edited by Clayborne Carson (New York: Warner Books, 1998) 9.

56 John Lewis, *Walking with the Wind: A Memoir of the Movement* (New York: Simon & Schuster, 1998) 327.

57 Thornton Dial, "Tribute to John Lewis: Remarks Given on September 9, 2005", www.gasupreme.us/pdf/john_lewis_speech.pdf.

58 Lester Maddox, "Pickrick Says," *Atlanta Journal,* May 18, 1963, 3.

59 Mayor William B. Hartsfield coined this phrase to emphasize that Atlanta, with all its rapid population and economic growth, was "a city too busy to hate."

60 "Divided City," *Time* 81/3 (January 18, 1963): 22.

61 Ivan Allen, Jr., *Mayor: Notes on the Sixties* (New York: Simon & Schuster, 1971) 72.

62 Ibid.

63 Reprinted in Clayborne Carson, ed., *The Movement, 1964–1970* (Westport CT: Greenwood Press, 1993) 314.

64 S. A. Reid, "Young: Statue symbol of Atlanta's greatness," April 15, 2008, B1, 5.

Index of Sites
with GPS Coordinates

Available at www.waypoints.net/sacredplaces

Tour 1: Auburn Avnue

175

SACRED PLACES

Tour 3: Martin Luther King, Jr. Drive

SACRED PLACES

Tour 4: Four Scattered Sites

Epilogue

SACRED PLACES

Area Transit Stations (MARTA)

M Five Points
30 Alabama Street SW; Atlanta GA 30303
33°45'14.00"N; 84°23'29.82"W

N1 Peachtree Center
216 Peachtree Street, NE; Atlanta GA 30303
33°45'29.83"N; 84°23'14.61"W

N2 Civic Center
435 West Peachtree St., NW, Atlanta GA 30308
33°46'2.71"N; 84°23'14.42"W

N4 Midtown
41 Tenth Street, NE; Atlanta GA 30309
33°46'45.75"N; 84°23'10.81"W

S2 West End
680 Lee Street, SW; Atlanta GA 30310
33°44'9.96"N; 84°24'49.29"W

E2 King Memorial
377 Decatur Street, SE; Atlanta GA 30312
33°44'59.85"N; 84°22'31.66"W

E3 Inman Park/Reynoldstown
1055 DeKalb Avenue, NE; Atlanta GA 30307
33° 84°21'9.02"W 84°21'9.02"W

W2 Vine City
502 Rhodes Street, NW; Atlanta GA 30314
33°45'23.84"N; 84°24'18.09"W

W3 Ashby
65 Joseph E. Lowery Blvd. Atlanta GA 30314
33°45'22.56"N; 84°25'1.23"W

W5 Hamilton E. Holmes
70 Hamilton E. Holmes Drive, NW Atlanta GA 30311
33°45'16.12"N; 84°28'12.57"W

Map Index

General Index

Photograph Credits

Ministers Sitting in Jail, p. 19. (Courtesy of AP/Wide World Photos)

Carnegie Library, p. 21. (Courtesy of Special Collections Department, Atlanta-Fulton Public Library System)

Irene Dobbs Jackson Speaking at Spelman, p. 23. (Courtesy of Spelman College Archives)

Yates & Milton Drugstore (Fair Street), p. 24. (Courtesy of Spelman College Archives)

"Atlanta Wall", p. 35. (Courtesy of *Atlanta Inquirer*)

Winding Line of Mourners Filing into Sisters Chapel, p. 92. (Courtesy of CORBIS Corporation)

Martin Luther King, Jr., Casket on Steps of Harkness Hall, p. 99. (Courtesy of The Museum of Fine Arts, Houston; Gift of Dr. Sarah Trotty, Joan Morgenstern, and Clinton T. Willour)

Arrest at Rich's, p. 112. (Courtesy of AP/Wide World Photos)

Sitting Down at Rich's Mural, p. 113. (Courtesy of artist Mike Mandel and photographer Stephen C. Traves)

SNCC Office, 6–8½ Raymond St., p. 123. (Courtesy of Danny Lyon)

Pickrick Restaurant (1950s), p. 139. (Postcard. Photographer unknown)

"Atlanta Wall", p. 141. (Courtesy of *Atlanta Inquirer*)

Protest Against the "Atlanta Wall", p. 144. (Courtesy of CORBIS Corporation)

Ruby Doris Smith Mug Shot, p. 146. (Courtesy of the Mississippi Department of Archives and History)

Ruby Doris Smith Robinson, p. 147. (Courtesy of Julius Lester)

All the other photographs were taken by co-author Harry G. Lefever.

About the Authors

HARRY G. LEFEVER is professor emeritus of sociology at Spelman College in Atlanta, Georgia. He has been a member of the Spelman College faculty since 1966 and served as chair of the Sociology Department (now Sociology and Anthropology) from 1975–1992. He has a BA from Eastern Mennonite College (1955), a MA from the University of Chicago (1962), and a PhD from Emory University (1971). Prior to coming to Spelman he taught for three years at Eastern Mennonite College in Harrisonburg, Virginia.

Lefever's research has focused on topics of sociology of religion, urban ethnography, urban cultural history, the history and cultures of the Caribbean and Central America, and the civil rights movement in the United States. He has published two books, *Turtle Bogue: Afro-Caribbean Life and Culture in a Costa Rican Village* (Susquehanna University Press, 1992), and *Undaunted By The Fight: Spelman College and the Civil Rights Movement, 1957–1967* (Mercer University Press, 2005), and numerous articles in scholarly journals. Lefever, the father of four children, lives in Atlanta.

MICHAEL C. PAGE serves as the geospatial librarian at Emory Libraries and as adjunct faculty to the Department of Environmental Studies at Emory University in Atlanta, Georgia. He has BA and MA degrees in geography from Georgia State University, where his master's research examined current planning and development efforts to retrofit suburban downtown landscapes and explored the ways in which such places could gain a greater sense of community, place, and identity. Page's research interests include cartography and information design, urban geography, field methods, and geospatial technologies. Page, an Atlanta native, resides in Atlanta with his wife and four children.